concrete5 Cookbook

Over 140 recipes to help you develop websites using the concrete5 content management system

David Strack

PUBLISHING

BIRMINGHAM - MUMBAI

concrete5 Cookbook

First published: July 2013

Production Reference: 1190713

Published by Packt Publishing Ltd.
Livery Place
35 Livery Street
Birmingham B3 2PB, UK.

ISBN 978-1-78216-454-8

www.packtpub.com

Cover Image by John M. Quick (john.m.quick@gmail.com)

Credits

Author

David Strack

Reviewers

Remo Laubacher

Werner Nindl

Sharon L. Rivera

James Shannon

Acquisition Editor

Joanne Fitzpatrick

Lead Technical Editor

Balaji Naidu

Technical Editors

Dipika Gaonkar

Dennis John

Athira Laji

Mrunmayee Patil

Sonali S. Vernekar

Project Coordinator

Shiksha Chaturvedi

Proofreader

Ting Baker

Indexer

Monica Ajmera Mehta

Production Coordinator

Arvindkumar Gupta

Cover Work

Arvindkumar Gupta

About the Author

David Strack has been a software engineer for over 10 years. With a strong background in HTML, PHP, and JavaScript, he has developed websites for dozens of companies, large and small. David currently works for a small startup in California creating energy analytics software. He lives in Milwaukee, Wisconsin, with his wife, Sarah, and their crazy dog, Brewski. David can usually be found hacking away with JavaScript, designing mobile apps, watching pro football, and drinking craft beer.

Thanks to my fantastic wife, Sarah, for her patience and support while I wrote this book. Also, thanks to the multitude of editors and reviewers; this book would not have been possible without them.

About the Reviewers

Remo Laubacher grew up in Central Switzerland in a small village surrounded by mountains and natural beauty. He started working with computers a long time ago and then, after various computer-related projects, focused on ERP and Oracle development.

After completing his BSc in Business Administration, Remo became a partner at Ortic, his ERP and Oracle business, as well as a partner at mesch web consulting and design GmbH. At mesch—where he's responsible for all development-related topics—he discovered concrete5 as the perfect tool for their web-related projects and has since become a key member of the concrete5 community. You can find his latest publications on `http://www.codeblog.ch/`. He is also the author of three books published by *Packt Publishing*: *concrete5 Beginner's Guide*, *concrete5 Beginner's Guide – Second Edition*, and *Creating concrete5 Themes*.

Werner Nindl is an Oracle Hyperion consultant by day and a concrete5 web developer by night. As a consultant he has lived and worked in Europe, China, and the US. During his day job, Werner manages consulting programs for financial consolidation and reporting.

Intrigued by the capabilities of concrete5 he has started to convert his clients' websites to concrete5. Participating in the review of this book has helped him to plan for future enhancements; and he believes that he can implement those enhancements now at a much lower resource cost then previously planned.

I want to thank the publishers for the opportunity to participate. Above all, I want to compliment Remo on his tremendous insight and knowledge about concrete5.

Sharon L. Rivera has attained the expert level in Business Intelligence Reporting Development. She has worked with legacy systems, North America-wide intranets, and corporate teams in developing Business Intelligence solutions.

She currently acts as a consultant and business developer for independent businesses.

James Shannon has been actively developing with concrete5 since its early days. He's contributed to the core and built a number of concrete5-powered sites, but mostly uses it as a framework to build complex web applications. Additionally, he's released a handful of popular packages that augment the core functionality of concrete5. More generally, he's been developing websites for 15 years using a number of technologies.

James' professional expertise is in strategic project management and change management.

James grew up in Southern California and graduated from UC Berkeley. He collects certifications; the most recent being the one that allows him to fly planes, and one that helps him manage projects.

> I'd like to thank the person most important to me, Julie Talone, and the one most important to her, Henry.

www.PacktPub.com

Support files, eBooks, discount offers and more

You might want to visit `www.PacktPub.com` for support files and downloads related to your book.

Did you know that Packt offers eBook versions of every book published, with PDF and ePub files available? You can upgrade to the eBook version at `www.PacktPub.com` and as a print book customer, you are entitled to a discount on the eBook copy. Get in touch with us at `service@packtpub.com` for more details.

At `www.PacktPub.com`, you can also read a collection of free technical articles, sign up for a range of free newsletters and receive exclusive discounts and offers on Packt books and eBooks.

`http://PacktLib.PacktPub.com`

Do you need instant solutions to your IT questions? PacktLib is Packt's online digital book library. Here, you can access, read and search across Packt's entire library of books.

Why Subscribe?

- Fully searchable across every book published by Packt
- Copy and paste, print and bookmark content
- On demand and accessible via web browser

Free Access for Packt account holders

If you have an account with Packt at `www.PacktPub.com`, you can use this to access PacktLib today and view nine entirely free books. Simply use your login credentials for immediate access.

Table of Contents

Preface

concrete5 is an increasingly popular open source content management system. concrete5 sets itself apart from other CMS applications with its easy to use point-and-click interface and multitude of features. Web developers love concrete5 because it is very easy to customize and build additional features in a relatively short time. This book aims to explain a variety of common programming tasks for concrete5 developers in an easy to read recipe format.

What this book covers

Chapter 1, *Pages and Page Types*, helps us learn how to work with pages and page types using the concrete5 API.

Chapter 2, *Working with Blocks*, creates custom block types and integrates blocks in your own website.

Chapter 3, *Files and File Sets*, develops files store in concrete5's excellent file manager.

Chapter 4, *Using the Core Helpers*, discovers the plethora of core helper files that come included with concrete5.

Chapter 5, *Working with Databases and Models*, explores the backbone of custom concrete5 development by working through database access and learning how to use models.

Chapter 6, *Creating CRUD Interfaces*, works through a bunch of useful recipes and creates interfaces to manage custom data in concrete5.

Chapter 7, *Working with Users and Permissions*, takes advantage of concrete5's user and permission model in your own applications and websites.

Chapter 8, *Working with Themes and Add-ons*, helps us learn how to create custom themes and add-ons, further expanding your concrete5 development skills.

Chapter 9, *System Events and Advanced Configuration*, uncovers concrete5's powerful developer functionality using advanced configuration settings and by hooking into system events.

Appendix A, Blueprint – Creating an Image Gallery Add-on, starts from scratch and builds an add-on that displays images stored in the file manager.

Appendix B, Blueprint – Creating an Events Calendar Add-on, combines all of the knowledge learned in previous chapters to create a fully functioning calendar add-on, complete with a CRUD interface and custom block type.

Appendix C, Submitting an Add-on Package to the concrete5 Marketplace, helps us to learn about the process that developers must follow to get their add-ons included in the concrete5 marketplace.

What you need for this book

Readers will need a copy of concrete5 running on a development (not production) server. This will allow readers to experiment with many different elements of the concrete5 API without disrupting normal website operation.

Readers will also need a code editor that is capable of editing the PHP files. This can be something like an advanced editor such as Adobe Dreamweaver or a basic text editor, such as Vim.

Some chapters also deal with browsing and querying MySQL databases, so a query browsing tool is recommended. HeidiSQL (on Windows), Sequel Pro (on OS X), and MySQL Workbench (all platforms) are some great tools that provide advanced functionality while browsing databases.

Who this book is for

This book is for beginner to intermediate PHP developers who would like to get to know concrete5 better, or for concrete5 veterans who would like to have a handy desk reference of the concrete5 API.

Conventions

In this book, you will find a number of styles of text that distinguish between different kinds of information. Here are some examples of these styles, and an explanation of their meaning.

Code words in text are shown as follows: " The Left Sidebar page type, for example, would have a handle of `left_sidebar`."

A block of code is set as follows:

```
function my_debug($var) {
   echo '<pre>';
   print_r($var);
   echo '</pre>';
   exit;
}
```

New terms and **important words** are shown in bold. Words that you see on the screen, in menus or dialog boxes for example, appear in the text like this: "clicking the **Next** button moves you to the next screen".

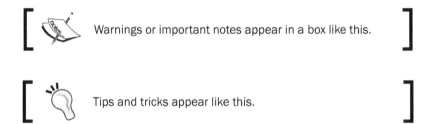

Warnings or important notes appear in a box like this.

Tips and tricks appear like this.

Reader feedback

Feedback from our readers is always welcome. Let us know what you think about this book—what you liked or may have disliked. Reader feedback is important for us to develop titles that you really get the most out of.

To send us general feedback, simply send an e-mail to feedback@packtpub.com, and mention the book title via the subject of your message.

If there is a topic that you have expertise in and you are interested in either writing or contributing to a book, see our author guide on www.packtpub.com/authors.

Customer support

Now that you are the proud owner of a Packt book, we have a number of things to help you to get the most from your purchase.

Downloading the example code

You can download the example code files for all Packt books you have purchased from your account at http://www.packtpub.com. If you purchased this book elsewhere, you can visit http://www.packtpub.com/support and register to have the files e-mailed directly to you.

Errata

Although we have taken every care to ensure the accuracy of our content, mistakes do happen. If you find a mistake in one of our books—maybe a mistake in the text or the code—we would be grateful if you would report this to us. By doing so, you can save other readers from frustration and help us improve subsequent versions of this book. If you find any errata, please report them by visiting `http://www.packtpub.com/submit-errata`, selecting your book, clicking on the **errata submission form** link, and entering the details of your errata. Once your errata are verified, your submission will be accepted and the errata will be uploaded on our website, or added to any list of existing errata, under the Errata section of that title. Any existing errata can be viewed by selecting your title from `http://www.packtpub.com/support`.

Piracy

Piracy of copyright material on the Internet is an ongoing problem across all media. At Packt, we take the protection of our copyright and licenses very seriously. If you come across any illegal copies of our works, in any form, on the Internet, please provide us with the location address or website name immediately so that we can pursue a remedy.

Please contact us at `copyright@packtpub.com` with a link to the suspected pirated material.

We appreciate your help in protecting our authors, and our ability to bring you valuable content.

Questions

You can contact us at `questions@packtpub.com` if you are having a problem with any aspect of the book, and we will do our best to address it.

1
Pages and Page Types

In this chapter we will cover the following topics:

- ▶ Getting the current Page object
- ▶ Getting a Page object by its ID
- ▶ Getting a Page object by its path
- ▶ Getting a Page type by its ID
- ▶ Getting a Page type by its handle
- ▶ Getting a page type's ID
- ▶ Getting a page type's name
- ▶ Getting a page type's handle
- ▶ Getting the icon for a page type
- ▶ Getting a list of pages that belong to a page type
- ▶ Creating a page type
- ▶ Updating a page type
- ▶ Deleting a page type
- ▶ Creating a page type
- ▶ Updating an existing page
- ▶ Setting page attributes
- ▶ Getting a page attribute
- ▶ Getting a page's ID
- ▶ Getting a page's path
- ▶ Getting a page's handle
- ▶ Getting a page's name

- ▸ Getting a page's description
- ▸ Getting a page's page type ID
- ▸ Getting a page's page type handle

- ▸ Getting a page's theme object
- ▸ Getting the children below a page
- ▸ Moving a page
- ▸ Deleting a page (and its children)
- ▸ Getting a list of pages
- ▸ Adding a page selector field to a form

Introduction

At the center of almost any content management system is the concept of pages. **concrete5** pages contain reusable portions of content called **blocks**. Blocks can contain anything from formatted text content that you enter yourself, to photo slideshows, to videos, to custom forms that you have developed that contain special functionality. concrete5 pages are extensions of the internal `Collection` object, which gets its name from the fact that it contains a collection of blocks that make up the page.

Since pages on a website usually contain repeating areas of information (perhaps a sidebar with some persistent widgets), concrete5 includes the concept of page types. Page types allow you to define different templates for creating new pages in concrete5. They are used to specify a default set of blocks, content, and special attributes that are added to new pages of that type, as well as to create different visual layouts through the concrete5 website.

A common page type would be **Left Sidebar**, which contains a list of links in the sidebar with an area to add blocks of content on the right. A normal concrete5 installation comes with a few default page types out of the box, including Left Sidebar and Full Width. In code, page types are referred to either by their unique numerical ID in the database, or more commonly, a human readable identifier called a **handle**. The Left Sidebar page type, for example, would have a handle of `left_sidebar`.

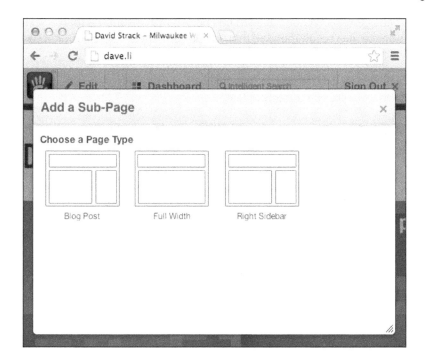

When adding pages to a concrete5 website through the user interface, you will likely notice that the first step is choosing a page type. Page types are also used by the Composer feature of concrete5, which can assist in creating several pages of the same type (such as blog posts).

There are two types of pages in concrete5, the first being a standard page that gets added to the sitemap and gets assigned a page type, and the second a **single page**, which is handled a bit differently and does not get assigned a page type. This chapter will deal with pages of the first type.

A note about the code in this chapter

Typically, you will write code that interacts with pages and page types in a block, a controller, or a model in your concrete5 application. For the purpose of these demonstrations, you can place the code anywhere where concrete5 lets you execute arbitrary PHP code.

A great place for this is to add a `site_process.php` or `site_post.php` file to your site's root `/config` directory. concrete5 will execute all of the code in that file once all of the core classes and libraries have been loaded (`site_post` gets executed before the current page has been loaded, `site_process` gets executed after the current page has been set). We will use classic PHP debugging techniques to verify that our code is working. Typically, we will dump the contents of a variable using PHP's `var_dump` or `print_r` functions followed by an `exit` command.

Because the debugging techniques used in this book can interrupt the regular functionality of a concrete5 website, it is recommended that you perform these exercises on a development copy of concrete5.

Be sure to comment out or remove the debugging code once you are finished, to resume the normal functionality of your concrete5 website.

Create a custom debugging function

To aid in the dumping of variables, we can create a simple debugging function that will wrap our output in `<pre>` tags and automatically `exit` for us.

Place the following code at the top of `/config/site_post.php` (create the file if it does not exist):

```
function my_debug($var) {
    echo '<pre>';
    print_r($var);
    echo '</pre>';
    exit;
}
```

Downloading the example code

You can download the example code files for all Packt books you have purchased from your account at `http://www.packtpub.com`. If you purchased this book elsewhere, you can visit `http://www.packtpub.com/support` and register to have the files e-mailed directly to you.

Now, when we wish to inspect the contents of a variable or other object, we can simply call `my_debug($variable)`, and get a nicely formatted, easy to read response.

Of course, you are more than welcome to use your own techniques for debugging variables.

Getting the current Page object

A very common task for concrete5 developers is to retrieve information from the page that is currently displayed. You will encounter this situation quite often, whether you need to update some information about the current page (such as a page title), check the current user's permissions on this page, or just display the page title. Fortunately, this is quite simple.

How to do it...

The steps for getting the current `Page` objects are as follows:

1. Create `/config/site_process.php` if it does not exist.
2. Open `/config/site_process.php` in your preferred text editor.
3. We can get the current `Page` object by calling the getCurrentPage static function of the Page class.

   ```
   $currentPage = Page::getCurrentPage();
   ```

4. If we inspect the contents of the `$currentPage` variable, we can see that it is a `Page` object, and now we are ready to perform further operations on it. In this example we are using our custom debugging function that was created in the chapter introduction.

   ```
   my_debug($currentPage);
   ```

How it works...

Calling the static `getCurrentPage` function on the `Page` class will look in the concrete5 `Request` object to get the current page. If that is not set, concrete5 will use the global `$c` variable. Note the use of `site_process.php` to dump the current page variable. We used this file because it is read after concrete5 has set the current `Page` object. Using `site_post.php` would have resulted in a null object.

There's more...

You may have already noticed that sometimes developers will use the global variable, `$c`, within their code to get the current `Collection` or `Page` object. This typically works fine, but best practices would be to use the `getCurrentPage` function to handle this for you.

See also

- ▸ The *Getting a Page object by its ID* recipe
- ▸ The *Getting a Page object by its path* recipe

Getting a Page object by its ID

In many situations, you will need to load a `Page` object using its unique numerical ID from the database. As mentioned earlier, pages are actually extensions of the `Collection` object, so you will actually be loading the page by its collection ID.

Getting ready

We will need to know the numerical ID of the page that you are attempting to load. Often this will be stored in other objects, perhaps even a custom entity that you have stored in the database. For example, say you have a recipes table in the database, and each recipe has its own page in the concrete5 website. You store the page ID for each recipe, so you can load the relevant `Page` object whenever necessary.

How to do it...

First you will have to get the page ID for the `Page` object that you are trying to load. For this example, we will just hard-code the ID of the page that we are loading. The steps are as follows:

1. Open `/config/site_post.php` in your favorite code editor.

2. First, let's store the ID of the page we are loading into a variable. In real-world use, you will likely have this ID stored in a database table, or available from some other code that you have run. The ID of the home page in concrete5 defaults to 1, so we will use that for our page's ID:

    ```
    $pageId = 1; // load the home page
    ```

3. Now that we have the ID of the page that we need to load, use the `getByID` function to get the `Page` object that we need:

    ```
    $page = Page::getByID($pageId);
    ```

4. We can inspect the `$page` variable and verify that it contains a `Page` object.

    ```
    my_debug($page);
    ```

How it works...

The page ID (also known as collection ID) is unique in the database, so calling the `getByID` function will load the correct page data and return a `Page` object that you can interact with.

See also

> ▸ The *Getting the current Page object* recipe
> ▸ The *Getting a Page object by its path* recipe

Getting a Page object by its path

concrete5 also supports the loading of `Page` objects by the path that is displayed in the web browser. This is a convenient way to load pages without knowing their numerical ID. In this exercise, we will load an About Us page by its path.

Getting ready

We will be loading a page with the path of `/about-us`. If this page does not exist in your concrete5 site, please add it to the sitemap before attempting this exercise.

How to do it...

Using a static function called `getByPath`, we can easily get a `Page` object without knowing the ID. The steps are as follows:

1. Open the `/config/site-post.php` file in your code editor.
2. Declare the path of the page that you wish to load.

   ```
   $path = '/about-us';
   ```

3. We can load the page located at `http://example.com/about-us` by passing the path string to the `getByPath` function.

   ```
   $aboutPage = Page::getByPath($path);
   ```

4. To make sure we grabbed the correct page, dump the `$aboutPage` variable to verify that we have a fully loaded `Page` object. We will use the custom debug function that we created in the chapter introduction.

   ```
   my_debug($aboutPage);
   ```

How it works...

concrete5 will query the database for the page that has the specified path assigned to it. You will want to use good judgment when loading pages by their paths, as that data can change easily through the concrete5 interface. Imagine that you are working on a site with 15 editors, and any one of them has the ability to edit the path of a page. concrete5 by default will save old page paths whenever a new one is changed, but it is not required. Hard coding page paths in your custom applications should be used only when appropriate. It is a much better idea to load pages by their ID whenever possible, as that ID does not change.

There's more...

You can load any page on the site using this technique. To load a `Careers` page that exists below the `About` page that we just loaded, you would write the following:

```
$careersPage = Page::getByPath('/about-us/careers');
```

You should know that concrete5 will cache the page IDs related to each path, so if you are experiencing unexpected results while using this function, make sure to clear your site cache by visiting `/dashboard/system/optimization/clear_cache/` on your concrete5 website.

See also

- The *Getting the current Page object* recipe
- The *Getting a Page object by its ID* recipe

Getting a page type by its ID

When creating and editing pages in concrete5 development, you will inevitably need to load the desired page type object that will be assigned to a page. Note that page types are actually instances of the `CollectionType` object in code. For consistency, we will continue to refer to them as page types outside of code.

Getting ready

We will continue performing these examples in the `/config/site-post.php` file, as that is a quick and easy place to run the arbitrary code. We will also continue making use of our custom `my_debug` function that was defined in the chapter introduction.

In this recipe, we will be loading a page type with the ID of `4`. Please make sure that this page type exists in your instance of concrete5, otherwise change the ID to something appropriate to your environment.

How to do it...

Much like loading pages, you will need to call a static function on the `CollectionType` class. The steps are as follows:

1. Open `/config/site_post.php` in your text editor.

2. First, we will need to know the numerical ID of the page type. In this case, we are going to assume that a page type called "Left Sidebar" exists, and that it has the numerical ID of `4`.

   ```
   $leftSidebarId = 4;
   ```

3. Now that we have the ID of the page type that we wish to load, we can call the `getByID` function of the `CollectionType` class.

   ```
   $leftSidebarPageType = CollectionType::getByID($leftSidebarId);
   ```

4. We can verify that we loaded the correct page type by inspecting the `$leftSidebarPageType` variable and verifying that it is an instance of the `CollectionType` class.

   ```
   my_debug($leftSidebarPageType);
   ```

How it works...

The `getByID` function performs a simple database query to find the page type that belongs to that ID. A `CollectionType` object is returned when a successful lookup is made.

See also

▸ The *Getting a page type by its handle* recipe

Getting a page type by its handle

As mentioned in the chapter introduction, page types also have human readable handles, which offer a convenient way of loading page types without knowing their numerical IDs. Handles are always alphanumerical strings with underscores between words, and do not contain any file extensions such as `.php`. For example, the handle for a page type called "Left Sidebar" would most likely be `left_sidebar`, but concrete5 lets users specify any alphanumeric string for a handle, so it's possible that the handle for Left Sidebar would also just be `left`.

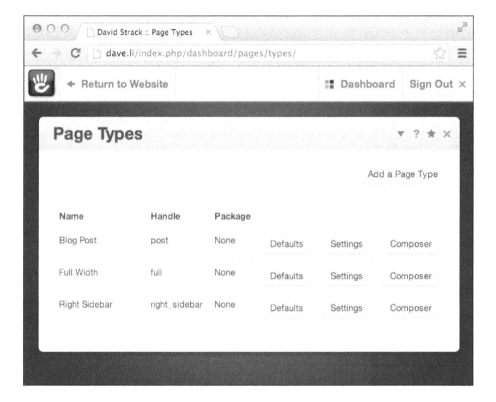

You can find the handles of page types by visiting the **Page Types** area of the concrete5 dashboard, located at `/dashboard/pages/types/` on your concrete5 website.

Getting ready

In this recipe, we will be loading a page type with the handle of `left_sidebar`. Please make sure that page type exists in your concrete5 installation, otherwise you can add a new page type with that handle, or adapt the recipe to work for your situation.

How to do it...

Here's how we would load the page type with a handle of `left_sidebar`. This is similar to loading a page by its path. The steps are as follows:

1. Open `/config/site_post.php` in your preferred code editor.

2. Declare the handle of the page type that you wish to load.

   ```
   $handle = 'left_sidebar';
   ```

3. Load the page type using the handle that we just defined.

   ```
   $pageType = CollectionType::getByHandle($handle);
   ```

4. You can verify that you have loaded the page type by dumping the `$pageType` variable.

   ```
   my_debug($pageType);
   ```

How it works...

A simple database query is performed, which will return a `CollectionType` object if it is successful.

There's more...

Just like the warning for loading pages by their paths, you will want to exercise the same good judgment when loading page types by their handles. Since these handles are just strings that can be edited through the concrete5 interface, you will need to make sure that you aren't writing code that could break if one of the site editors changes the handle of a page type.

See also

▶ The *Getting a page type by its ID* recipe

Getting a page type's ID

Once a page type has been loaded, we can get different information from it. Sometimes, if a page type is loaded by its handle, or if it was provided from another function call, developers will need to get the page type's ID from an existing page type object. In this exercise, we will load a page type by its handle, and then find out the ID of the page type.

Getting ready

We will be loading a page type with a handle of `right_sidebar` in this example. If that page type does not exist in your concrete5 system, feel free to adapt this recipe to suit your specific situation.

How to do it...

The steps for getting a page type's ID are as follows:

1. Open `/config/site_post.php` in your code editor.
2. Load the page type by its path:

   ```
   $pageType = CollectionType::getByHandle('right_sidebar');
   ```

3. Get the ID from the page type.

   ```
   $id = $pageType->getCollectionTypeId();
   ```

4. Dump the page type ID (we are using the custom debugger explained in this chapter's introduction).

   ```
   my_debug($id);
   ```

How it works...

Once the page type object is loaded, developers can call a number of functions to retrieve data from it, including the numeric ID.

See also

  ▶   The *Getting a page type by its handle* recipe

Getting a page type's name

Page type objects also contain methods to retrieve the name of the page type. In this exercise, we will load a page type by its handle, and then retrieve the name of the page type.

Getting ready

We will be loading a page type with the handle of `right_sidebar`, so if that page type does not exist in your instance of concrete5, please adapt this recipe to suit your needs.

How to do it...

The steps for getting a page type's name are as follows:

1. Open `/config/site_post.php` in your preferred code editor.
2. Load the page type by its handle:

    ```
    $pageType = CollectionType::getByHandle('right_sidebar');
    ```

3. Get the name of the page type.

    ```
    $name = $pageType->getCollectionTypeName();
    ```

4. Dump the name using our custom debugger.

    ```
    my_debug($name);
    ```

How it works...

The `getCollectionTypeName` function simply returns the string value of the page type's name.

See also

- ▸ The *Getting a page type by its handle* recipe

Getting a page type's handle

If a page type has been loaded by its ID or has been provided in a different manner, developers may want to retrieve the handle of the page type. In this example, we will load a page type with an ID of 4 and use the concrete5 API to get its handle.

Getting ready

We will be loading a page type with an ID of 4, so please ensure that this exists in your concrete5 website. Feel free to change the ID in this recipe to something appropriate for your instance of concrete5.

How to do it...

The steps for getting a page type's handle are as follows:

1. Open `/config/site_post.php` in your preferred code editor.
2. Load the page type by its ID.

   ```
   $pageType = CollectionType::getByID(4);
   ```

3. Get the handle of the page type.

   ```
   $handle = $pageType->getCollectionTypeHandle();
   ```

4. Dump the handle using our custom debugger function.

   ```
   my_debug($handle);
   ```

How it works...

The function `getCollectionTypeHandle` of the page type object returns the handle string of the page type.

See also

▸ The *Getting a page type by its ID* recipe

Getting the icon for a page type

In the concrete5 dashboard interface, page types have icons associated with them. In some advanced applications, you may want to retrieve the icon for the page type. In this recipe, we will load a page type by its handle and get its icon.

Getting ready

We will be loading a page type with a handle of `right_sidebar`. Feel free to change this handle to something appropriate for your concrete5 instance if `right_sidebar` does not exist.

How to do it...

The steps for getting the icon for a page are as follows:

1. Open `/config/site_post.php` in your favorite code editor, as this is a good place to try out random code.

2. Load the page type by its path.

```
$pageType = CollectionType::getByHandle('right_sidebar');
```

3. Get the icon image.

```
$icon = $pageType->getCollectionTypeIconImage();
```

4. Output the image. You should see the icon's image appear.

```
echo $icon;
exit;
```

How it works...

concrete5 returns a string containing the actual HTML image tag with the collection type's icon.

There's more...

If you would like to get the numeric ID of the file containing the page type icon, you can simply call this function:

```
$iconId = $pageType->getCollectionTypeIcon();
```

The numeric ID is useful when working with the file manager in concrete5, which is discussed in detail in *Chapter 3*, *Files and File Sets* of this book.

See also

▶ The *Getting a page type by its ID* recipe

Getting a list of pages that belong to a page type

In many advanced concrete5 applications, developers may need to find a list of all of the pages that belong to a given page type. In this example, we will get an array of pages that have a page type with the handle of `right_sidebar`.

Getting ready

If your instance of concrete5 does not have a page type with the handle of `right_sidebar`, feel free to adapt the recipe to suit your needs. We will continue using `/config/site_post.php` as our sandbox to run random code snippets, as well as our custom debugging function that we created in this chapter's introduction.

How to do it...

The steps for getting a list of pages belonging to a page type are as follows:

1. Open `/config/site_post.php` in your code editor to try out the following code.
2. Load the page type by its handle.

   ```
   $pageType = CollectionType::getByHandle('right_sidebar');
   ```

3. Get the array of `Page` objects.

   ```
   $pages = $pageType->getPages();
   ```

4. Dump the array to see its contents.

   ```
   foreach ($pages as $page) {
     echo $page->getCollectionTitle().'<br />';
   }
   exit;
   ```

How it works...

concrete5 simply uses the relational MySQL database to find all of the pages that are related to the page type. Be aware that concrete5 ignores permissions settings when this function is called, so this should really only be used for internal purposes.

See also

▶ The *Getting a page type by its handle* recipe

Creating a page type

You can easily add new page types through the concrete5 user interface, but there are some situations that can require you to create page types dynamically using PHP code.

Getting ready

First, you will need to create an associative array that contains the data of the page type that you are creating.

The array can contain the following fields:

Attribute	Required?	Description
ctHandle	Yes	The collection type handle: an alphanumeric string with underscores between words.
ctName	Yes	The collection type name: a string that will appear in the concrete5 interface.
ctIcon	No	If you'd like to specify an icon for this page type, pass in the numerical ID of the icon from the File Manager.
ctIsInternal	No	A Boolean indicating if this page type is an internal page type. Internal page types do not appear in the page creation dialog in the concrete5 interface.
akID	No	An array of attribute key IDs to be added to the new page type.

How to do it...

We will create a page type using only the required fields: ctHandle and ctName. The steps are as follows:

1. Open /config/site_post.php in your preferred code editor.

2. Declare the handle of the new page type to be created.

   ```
   $handle = 'page_type_handle';
   ```

3. Declare the array that contains the data for the ctHandle and ctName fields.

   ```
   $data = array(
     'ctHandle' => $handle,
     'ctName' => 'Page Type Name'
   );
   ```

4. Check to see if the page type already exists by loading it by the new handle.

   ```
   $pageType = CollectionType::getByHandle($handle);
   ```

5. If the page type does not exist, create it.

```
if (!$pageType) {
  $newPageType = CollectionType::add($data);
}
```

6. If it does exist, assign the existing page type to the new page type variable.

```
else {
  $newPageType = $pageType;
}
```

7. Dump the new page type variable to ensure that it worked.

```
my_debug($newPageType);
```

How it works...

concrete5 will take the data array that you pass in and use it to create a new `CollectionType` record in the database. concrete5 will also automatically generate a Master Collection page in the database. The Master Collection is a template page that concrete5 will use as base for all pages of that type. Any blocks, attributes, or other data assigned to the Master Collection will automatically be added to any new pages created with that page type.

There's more...

If you are creating this page type in a custom package, you will need to pass in your package object to the `add()` function, so concrete5 knows that this page type belongs to your package. That way, when users uninstall your package, they will have the option of removing all of the page types that it created.

Assuming that you know the handle of your package, use the following code to create a page type with it:

```
$data = array(
  'ctHandle' => $handle,
  'ctName' => 'Page Type Name'
);
$pkg = Package::getByHandle('my_package');
$newPageType = CollectionType::add($data, $pkg);
```

See also

▸ The *Creating custom add-on package* recipe

▸ The *Updating a page type* recipe

Updating a page type

Updating page types is very similar to creating a page type as discussed in the previous recipe.

How to do it...

First you will need to load an existing page type. You will need to pass in the same data array when updating page types as you would when creating them. The steps are as follows:

1. Open `/config/site_post.php` in your code editor.

2. Declare the old handle and the new handle variables.

```
$handle = 'page_type_handle';
$newHandle = 'new_handle';
```

3. Define the new `$data` array with the new handle and new name.

```
$data = array(
   'ctHandle' => $newHandle,
   'ctName' => 'New Name'
);
```

4. If the page type exists, update it.

```
$pageType = CollectionType::getByHandle($handle);
if ($pageType) {
   $pageType->update($data);
}
```

5. Verify that the page type was updated by visiting `/dashboard/pages/types` in your concrete5 website.

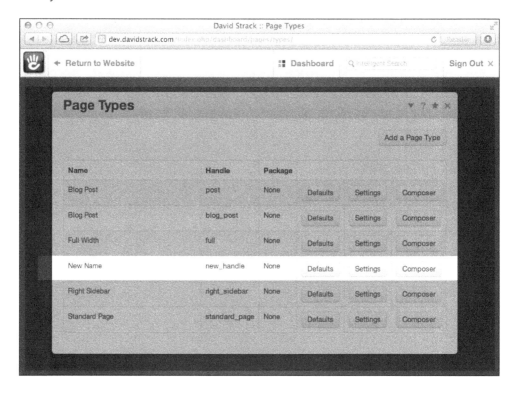

How it works...

concrete5 will update the record in the database for the loaded page type. The Master Collection page is not updated when this function is called. You also cannot pass a packaged object to the update function, as that is only necessary when first creating a page type.

See also

- ▸ The *Creating a page type* recipe
- ▸ The *Deleting a page type* recipe

Deleting a page type

In addition to adding and editing page types, you can also delete them.

Getting ready

Since deleting page types is a destructive action that is irreversible, it's a good idea to create a dummy page type with the handle of `delete_me` for this exercise. We will also continue using `site_post.php` to execute arbitrary code.

How to do it...

The steps for deleting a page type are as follows:

1. Open `/config/site_post.php` in your preferred code editor.
2. Define the handle of the page to be deleted.

   ```
   $handle = 'delete_me';
   ```

3. Load the page type by its handle.

   ```
   $pageType = CollectionType::getByHandle($handle);
   ```

4. Now, delete the page type.

   ```
   $pageType->delete();
   ```

How it works...

The `delete()` function deletes the page type, the Master Collection, and all of the pages that use it. Use this function very cautiously, as once the data has been deleted, it cannot be recovered (unless you have a backup copy of the site's database).

See also

- The *Getting a page type by its ID* recipe

Creating a page type

Creating pages dynamically is a central concept of concrete5 development and can unlock a lot of powerful features in custom applications. Imagine a concrete5 website that has a recipes database. You could make it so, that every time a recipe is added to the database, a new page for that recipe is added to the sitemap, immediately improving the depth of content on your website, its usability, and even search engine performance.

In this example, we will create an "About Us" page and add it to the sitemap.

Getting ready

We are continuing the practice of putting our code in `/config/site_post.php` for the purposes of demonstration and testing. In real-world use, your dynamic page creation would happen in controller files or in add-on packages.

We will be assigning the new page a page type with the handle of `right_sidebar`. If this doesn't exist in your own concrete5 installation, please adapt the recipe to suit your needs.

How to do it...

The steps for creating a page are as follows:

1. Open `/config/site_post.php` in your code editor.

2. Load the page type that the new page will use. We will load the page type using its handle (`right_sidebar`, in this case).

    ```
    $pageType = CollectionType::getByHandle('right_sidebar');
    ```

3. Create an associative array that contains the fields that you wish to specify for the new page. In this example, we will only specify the page's name and handle.

    ```
    $data = array(
      'cName' => 'About Us',
      'cHandle' => 'about'
    );
    ```

4. Load the parent page that the new page will be placed under. In this case, we are loading the home page, since the new page will be available at the top level.

    ```
    $parent = Page::getByID(1);
    ```

5. Add the page by passing the `$pageType` object and `$data` array to the add function of the parent `Page` class.

    ```
    $newPage = $parent->add($pageType, $data);
    ```

6. Output a message and exit the process.

```
echo 'done!';
exit;
```

7. Visit your site's homepage to execute the code in `site_post.php`.

8. If you see the success message, comment out the code in `site_post.php` so you can visit the newly created page. Otherwise, concrete5 will create a new page every time the site is loaded into a browser.

9. Visit the newly created page at `http://example.com/about`.

How it works...

The `add()` function is a wrapper for the `Collection` class's `add()` function. Calling it will create a new `Collection` record in the database, and a new pending `CollectionVersion` record (which will be approved if the `cvIsApproved` variable is set to `true` or left blank). Then the new page will inherit the necessary permissions and get all of the blocks and other attributes from the Master Collection of the related page type.

There's more...

You will need to provide two parameters to the `add()` function, a `CollectionType` object (which we worked with earlier in this chapter), and an associative array containing all of the data needed to create the page. The associative array can contain the following fields.

Attribute	Required?	Description
cName	Yes	This is the name of the page. This will be how the page is referred to throughout the site, and will be automatically used in the page's `<title>` tag (unless overridden by a meta title attribute, which you can specify after the page has been created.)
cHandle	No	This is the handle of the page, that is, how the page title will appear in the page URL. If you omit this field, concrete5 will generate a handle based off of the `cName` field. This is a little confusing, because concrete5 allows dash characters ("-") in page handles, but does not seem to support them anywhere else. This is good, though, because the typical convention for page paths on the web is to use dashes rather than underscores.

Attribute	Required?	Description
cDescription	No	This is the internal description of the page. It is just a string that describes the purpose of a page. Some themes might use this data somewhere in the theme, but it is not required. Older versions of concrete5 displayed the description of the page in the dashboard, but that has gone away since the update to version 5.5.
uID	No	This is an integer ID to indicate the page's author. Pass in the ID of any user in the concrete5 Users table to set that user as the page author. If omitted, the currently logged in user will be registered as the page author.
pkgID	No	This is an integer ID of the package that created this page. Make sure to include this field if you are creating pages from a package. If you omit this field, but the attached page type belongs to a package, the page type's package ID will be attached to this page. This will help users optionally remove any pages that were created by your package if they choose to uninstall your package.
cDatePublic	No	This is a MySQL-formatted date string (YYYY-MM-DD) of when this page should be publicly visible on the website. If omitted, the current date and time from the web server is used.
cvIsApproved	No	This is a Boolean that indicates if the initial page version should be approved. Defaults to true if nothing is specified. When pages are approved, they are made immediately visible to all users that have permission to access that page on the website. Any subsequent edits to a page will require the new versions of the page to be approved before users can see the changes.

See also

- The *Updating an existing page* recipe
- The *Getting a page type by its ID* recipe
- The *Getting a page type by its handle* recipe

Updating an existing page

Updating pages is similar to creating them in that you must first pass in an associative array containing all of the data that you wish to update on the page.

Getting ready

In this recipe, we will be modifying a page with the path of /about. We created that page in the previous recipe, but if it does not exist on your system, please adapt the code to your needs.

How to do it...

In this example, we will update the name of the About page. The steps are as follows:

1. First, we need to load the Page object by its path.

   ```
   $page = Page::getByPath('/about');
   ```

2. Create an associative array with the data that you wish to update.

   ```
   $data = array(
     'cName' => 'About Our Company'
   );
   ```

3. Pass the data array into the $page object's update function.

   ```
   $page->update($data);
   ```

4. Output a success message and exit the process.

   ```
   echo 'done!';
   exit;
   ```

How it works...

The update function updates the necessary tables in the database with the newly specified information. concrete5 will also rescan all permissions for this page and all of the related page paths. When the function is complete, the on_page_update event is fired, which you can write custom code to listen to and perform custom actions when a page is updated. Listening to system events is covered in a later chapter.

There's more...

Just like creating a page, you will need to pass an associative array to the `update()` function in order to update an existing page. You can use all of the fields specified in the previous recipe for adding a page, in addition to these other optional fields.

Attribute	Description
ctID	This is the numerical ID of a page type to change the page to. Supply this field to change the page type of a given page.
cCacheFullPageContent	A Boolean that specifies if the page should support full page caching (some block types do not support full page caching, so only use this when the blocks on that page offer full caching support).
cCacheFullPageContentOverrideLifetime	A string to tell concrete5 how the cache lifetime should perform. Possible values are default, custom, or forever.
cCacheFullPageContentLifetimeCustom	A setting in minutes as to how long the cache should last when the override mode is set to custom.

See also

▸ The *Creating a page type* recipe

Setting page attributes

Pages, like most objects in concrete5, can have any type of custom attribute attached to them. This allows for immense flexibility, but it can be difficult to read and write these attributes using raw SQL. The concrete5 API makes setting and reading page attributes easy.

Getting ready

You will need to know at least the handle of the attribute key that you wish to assign to the page. A common attribute to set is the `Meta Title` attribute, which updates the text that appears in the HTML `<title>` tag.

How to do it...

We will set the `Meta Title` attribute to the About Us page in this example. The steps are as follows:

1. Open `/config/site_post.php` in your preferred code editor.
2. Load the `Page` object that you wish to set the attribute on.

    ```
    $page = Page::getByPath('/about');
    ```

3. Call the `setAttribute` function on the `$page` object, passing in two parameters: the attribute handle (key), and the value.

    ```
    $page->setAttribute('meta_title', 'New Page Meta Title');
    ```

4. Output a success message and exit the process.

    ```
    echo 'done!';
    exit;
    ```

How it works...

The `setAttribute` function is a member of the `Collection` class, which the `Page` class extends. It requires that you provide two parameters, an attribute key (which can either be a string representing the attribute key handle (which we provided here), or an actual `AttributeKey` object), and the value.

There's more...

The `setAttribute` function is very handy for setting the data of any kind of page attribute. One can update a page's meta information (such as description, keywords, and title) and also give the page various options, such as, excluding it from the navigation (as seen previously) or from the `sitemap.xml` file that search engines look for.

You can update any attribute that has been installed in the concrete5 system. To see all available page attributes, or to create new ones, visit the **Page Attributes** area of your site's dashboard (located at `/dashboard/pages/attributes/`).

See also

-   The *Getting a page by its path* recipe
-   The *Getting a page attribute* recipe

Getting a page attribute

In addition to being able to set page attributes, developers can also retrieve attributes just as easily. In this exercise, we will get the `Meta Title` attribute for the About page.

Getting ready

We are assuming the presence of a page with the path of `/about` in this recipe. If that page does not exist, you can create it, or adapt the code in this recipe to fit your circumstances.

How to do it...

The steps for getting a page attribute are as follows:

1. Open `/config/site_post.php` in your preferred editor. This is a good place to run some arbitrary code.

2. Load the `Page` object.

   ```
   $page = Page::getByPath('/about');
   ```

3. Get the `meta_title` attribute.

   ```
   $title = $page->getAttribute('meta_title');
   ```

4. Dump the variable using the custom debugging function that we created in the chapter's introduction.

   ```
   my_debug($title);
   ```

How it works...

concrete5 uses the attribute handle string to find the appropriate record in the database and return its value. concrete5 stores attributes in the EAV format (**entity**, **attribute**, **value**), and this makes it difficult to read these values directly with SQL queries. The concrete5 API simplifies this for developers.

See also

- ▸ The *Getting a page by its path* recipe
- ▸ The *Setting a page attribute* recipe

Getting a page's ID

Developers will often need to know a page's ID, especially when relating pages to other database objects (such as a blog post or calendar event). In this example, we will load the /about page that we've been working with and get its ID.

Getting ready

Please make sure the /about page exists in your instance of concrete5. Feel free to modify the code in this recipe if that page does not exist.

How to do it...

The steps for getting a page's ID are as follows:

1. Open /config/site_post.php in your code editor.

2. Load the Page object by its path.

    ```
    $page = Page::getByPath('/about');
    ```

3. Get the page's ID.

    ```
    $id = $page->getCollectionId();
    ```

4. Dump the contents of the $id variable to see what the ID is.

    ```
    my_debug($id);
    ```

See also

▸   The *Getting a page by its path* recipe

Getting a page's path

In addition to being able to get a page's ID, developers can also retrieve the path for a page. In this recipe, we will load a page by its ID and then retrieve its path.

How to do it...

The steps for getting a page's path are as follows:

1. Open `/config/site_post.php` in your preferred code editor.
2. Load the page by its ID. We will use the ID of 4 here, which should belong to a page on the dashboard.

   ```
   $page = Page::getByID(4);
   ```

3. Get the page's path.

   ```
   $path = $page->getCollectionPath();
   ```

4. Use the custom debugging function to output the path.

   ```
   my_debug($path);
   ```

See also

▶ The *Getting a page by its ID* recipe

Getting a page's handle

Pages, like page types and other objects in concrete5, have handles in addition to paths. The handle is similar to a slug in other content management systems. In this exercise, we will load a page by its ID and then retrieve its handle.

How to do it...

The steps for getting a page's handle are as follows:

1. Open `/config/site_post.php` in your code editor.
2. Load the page by its ID.

   ```
   $page = Page::getByID(4);
   ```

3. Get the page's handle.

   ```
   $handle = $page->getCollectionHandle();
   ```

4. Dump the handle variable to see its contents.

   ```
   my_debug($handle);
   ```

See also

▸ The *Getting a page by its ID* recipe

Getting a page's name

Page names are often used as the de facto titles in concrete5. In this exercise, we will load a page by its path, and then get its name.

How to do it...

The steps for getting a page's name are as follows:

1. Open `/config/site_post.php` in your editor.

2. Load the page by its path.

   ```
   $page = Page::getByPath('/about');
   ```

3. Get the page's title.

   ```
   $name = $page->getCollectionName();
   ```

4. Dump the contents of the title variable.

   ```
   my_debug($name);
   ```

See also

▸ The *Getting a page by its path* recipe

Getting a page's description

Page descriptions are not used very widely used in concrete5. Some themes will treat them as content excerpts, while other add-ons will use descriptions as a generic attribute storage area. Regardless, they are still built into concrete5, and in this recipe we will load a page by its path and retrieve its description.

Getting ready

Many pages in concrete5 do not have descriptions. If you wish, you can edit a page to add a description as shown in the following screenshot:

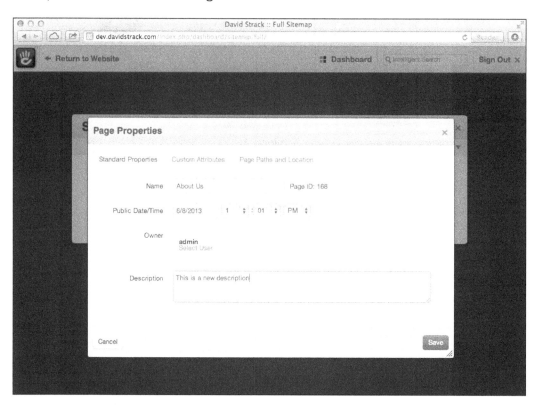

How to do it...

The steps for getting a page's description are as follows:

1. Open the `/config/site_post.php` file in your code editor.

2. Load the page by its path.

   ```
   $page = Page::getByPath('/about');
   ```

3. Get the page's description.

   ```
   $description = $page->getCollectionDescription();
   ```

4. Dump the contents of the description variable.

   ```
   my_debug($description);
   ```

See also

- ▸ The *Getting a page by its path* recipe

Getting a page's page type ID

As we discussed earlier in the chapter, pages are assigned a page type. In this recipe, we will get the page type ID from a `Page` object.

How to do it...

The steps for getting a page's page type ID are as follows:

1. Open `/config/site_post.php` in your code editor, so we can run some arbitrary code.

2. Load the page by its path.

   ```
   $page = Page::getByPath('/about');
   ```

3. Get the page type ID for this page.

   ```
   $pageTypeId = $page->getCollectionTypeID();
   ```

4. Dump the page type ID using our custom debugging function.

   ```
   my_debug($pageTypeId);
   ```

See also

- ▸ The *Getting a page by its path* recipe

Getting a page's page type handle

In addition to being able to retrieve the ID of a page's page type, developers can also get the handle.

How to do it...

The steps for getting a page's page type handle are as follows:

1. Open `/config/site_post.php` in your code editor, since we will just be running some arbitrary code.

2. Load the page by its path.

   ```
   $page = Page::getByPath('/about');
   ```

3. Get the page type handle.

```
$handle = $page->getCollectionTypeHandle();
```

4. Dump the handle variable to see its contents.

```
my_debug($handle);
```

See also

▶ The *Getting a page by its path* recipe

Getting a page's theme object

Every page can have its own individual theme in concrete5. While it's typical for most sites to only use one global theme, concrete5 does allow developers to set individual themes for each page. In this recipe, we will get the page's theme object, which can be used to see what theme is active on a given page.

How to do it...

The steps for getting a page's theme object are as follows:

1. Open `/config/site_post.php` in your preferred code editor.
2. Load the page by its path.

```
$page = Page::getByPath('/about');
```

3. Get the theme object.

```
$theme = $page->getCollectionThemeObject();
```

4. Dump the theme object to inspect the class.

```
my_debug($theme);
```

See also

▶ The *Getting a page by its path* recipe

Getting the children below a page

If you need to access the children of a page, you can have concrete5 return an array of numerical IDs. These IDs can then be used to load each of the `Page` objects individually.

How to do it...

The steps for getting the children below a page are as follows:

1. Open `/config/site_post.php` in your preferred code editor.
2. Load the parent page by its ID.

   ```
   $page = Page::getByID(1);
   ```

3. Get the array of child IDs.

   ```
   $children = $page->getCollectionChildrenArray();
   ```

4. Loop through the child ID array and output the name of each page.

   ```
   foreach ($children as $childId) {
     $child = Page::getByID($childId);
     echo $child->getCollectionName().'<br />';
   }
   ```

5. Exit the process.

   ```
   exit;
   ```

How it works...

concrete5 will return an array of numeric IDs for each of the pages beneath the parent page. In this example, we loaded the home page, so the result should be a list of every page on the website. This function ignores permissions, and can be taxing on the database if there are a lot of pages to load. It is a better idea to use the `PageList` class to loop through pages, and that class is described later on in this chapter.

Moving a page

The concrete5 sitemap is a great tool for managing the page hierarchy of your website. It lets you arrange the order of pages, and even drag-and-drop pages to different areas of the site. Thankfully, you aren't limited to using the graphical interface to move pages around the site. You can also rearrange pages dynamically in your custom concrete5 applications.

Getting ready

In this example, we are going to move a Careers page underneath the About Us page. Before we can move a page, we need to have the `Page` object of the new parent page that we are moving the current page to.

This exercise assumes that pages exist at both `/about` and `/careers` in your concrete5 site. You can create those pages through the concrete5 interface, or adapt the code in this recipe to work with pages that exist on your own site.

How to do it...

The steps for moving a page are as follows:

1. Open `/config/site_post.php`, as that is a safe place to play with some random code.

2. First, load the About Us page, which is where the Careers page will be moved to.

   ```
   $newParent = Page::getByPath('/about');
   ```

3. Now, we need to load the careers page that we are moving.

   ```
   $careersPage = Page::getByPath('/careers');
   ```

4. Finally, call the `move` function on the careers page, passing it the new parent page and an optional Boolean which tells concrete5 if we want to save the old page path as well as the new one.

   ```
   $careersPage->move($newParent, true);
   ```

How it works...

The move function is very easy to use. You only need to provide one parameter, which is a `Page` object of the new parent that you are moving the page under. There is an optional second parameter to indicate if you wish to retain the old page path in addition to the current one. That parameter defaults to false.

Once the page is moved, it will inherit the permissions of the new parent page (if the page does not have its own permissions set explicitly).

Once the page is moved, the event `on_page_move` is fired.

See also

- ▶ *Listening to system events* in Chapter 9, *System Events and Advanced Configuration*
- ▶ The *Getting a Page object by its path* recipe

Deleting a page (and its children)

concrete5 also makes it easy to delete pages from the sitemap.

Getting ready

Deleting pages is a permanent destructive action. When experimenting with this code, it would be a good idea to create a dummy page with a path of `/delete-me`.

How to do it...

We will permanently delete the about us page and all of its child pages. The steps are as follows:

1. First, load the page that you wish to delete. We will delete a dummy page.

   ```
   $page = Page::getByPath('/delete-me');
   ```

2. Call the `delete()` function on the `Page` object.

   ```
   $page->delete();
   ```

How it works...

concrete5 will fire the `on_page_delete` event before any actual deleting occurs. After the event fires, the page (and all of its children) are deleted from the database. This operation is permanent, so it is important to make sure that you only delete pages when you are certain that they are no longer needed.

There's more...

If you don't want to permanently delete a page, you can move it to the Trash. As of concrete5 version 5.5, pages can be "temporarily" deleted and moved under a special internal page called the Trash.

```
$page->moveToTrash();
```

See also

▸ The *Getting a page by its path* recipe

Getting a list of pages

Many applications will have a need to get a list of pages and perform various filter and sorting functions on the list. For this, there is the `PageList` class, which exposes many convenient helper functions to assist in working with large lists of pages.

Getting ready

In this example, we are going to find all of the pages under the `/blog` page. This is a common use of the page list model. The `PageList` class is not automatically loaded by concrete5, so we will need to use the `Loader` class to have it available to us.

If your site does not have a page located at `/blog`, it would be helpful to create that page, as well as a few child pages below it. Otherwise, feel free to adapt the code in this recipe to suit your needs.

How to do it...

In this recipe, we will get a list of 20 pages that exist under `/blog` in the sitemap. The steps are as follows:

1. First, we must make the `PageList` class available for us to use.

   ```
   Loader::model('page_list');
   ```

2. Create a new instance of the `PageList` class. We will assign it to a variable called `$list`.

   ```
   $list = new PageList();
   ```

3. Filter the list to only include pages underneath the `/blog` page.

   ```
   $list->filterByPath('/blog');
   ```

4. Limit the list of pages to only include the first 20 results.

   ```
   $list->setItemsPerPage(20);
   ```

5. Run the database query and get the first "page" of results, which will return an array of 20 `Page` objects.

   ```
   $pages = $list->getPage();
   ```

6. Dump the contents of the pages variable to see the array.

   ```
   foreach ($pages as $page) {
     echo $page->getCollectionTitle().'<br />';
   }
   exit;
   ```

How it works...

The `PageList` class extends the core `DatabaseItemList` class, which has a number of useful functions itself. The `get()` function accepts two parameters, the number of records to retrieve, and the offset.

There's more...

The page list class implements "magic methods," which allow allow us to filter the list by any page attribute. We simply need to create a function name based off of the camel cased version of the attribute handle, preceded by "filterBy". So to filter all pages that have the `exclude_nav` attribute, we would write the following function:

```
$list->filterByExcludeNav(true);
```

Alternatively, if you want to just get an array of the first 99 `Page` objects and ignore pagination, use the `get()` function.

```
$pages = $list->get(99);
```

Since version 5.5, concrete5 uses Twitter's open source Bootstrap CSS framework for many of their internal styles. You can get the pagination controls in nicely formatted HTML (with relevant Bootstrap CSS classes) by printing/echoing the results of the following function (preferably you'd use this function in a view or template file of a block or single page):

```
echo $list->displayPagingV2();
```

The `DatabaseItemList` class and `PageList` class have several functions that make working with a collection of pages easier. You can filter by keywords, by collection type, parent page, and by any attribute using magic methods. We will cover the `DatabaseItemList` class further in *Chapter 5*, *Working with Databases and Models*.

Adding a page selector field to a form

It is easy to add a page selector field to a form. When clicked on, the sitemap will appear in a modal window, allowing for easy browsing and selecting of a page. This allows for user friendly custom applications that can allow users to attach pages to any type of custom object, like a blog post or cooking recipe, for example.

Getting ready

We will need to use the `FormPageSelectorHelper` class, which we will need to load using the `Loader` library.

This recipe will need to be written inside of an HTML form somewhere in your site. We have created a basic single page for this purpose, which can be downloaded with the code from the website for this book. To install the single page, copy the code for this recipe to your concrete5 site directory and visit `/dashboard/pages/single`. Add a new single page with a path of `/example`.

How to do it...

concrete5 includes a helper to generate the necessary JavaScript and HTML text needed to show the sitemap selector widget. We will use the `Loader` class to include and return the `PageSelectorHelper` class, which will then return the entire HTML that we need. The steps are as follows:

1. Make the `pageSelector` helper class available for us to use. The `Loader` class will automatically instantiate and return the instantiated helper object when the helper gets loaded.

   ```
   $pageSelector = Loader::helper('form/page_selector');
   ```

2. Output the HTML and JavaScript required allowing users to select a page.

   ```
   echo $pageSelector->selectPage('page_id');
   ```

How it works...

The `selectPage` function returns the HTML and JavaScript necessary to produce a page selector field. There is only one parameter required, and that is a string indicating the name of the field. concrete5 will add a hidden `<input>` element to the form, which will allow the selected page ID to be read from a POST request.

In this example, once the form is submitted, you could retrieve the selected page ID by looking in the `$_POST` super variable.

```
$pageId = $_POST['page_id'];
```

There's more...

You can specify a page ID in the optional second parameter, which will populate the page selector with an existing page.

```
$page = Page::getByCollectionPath('/about-us');
echo $pageSelector->selectPage('page_id', $page-
    >getCollectionID());
```

The `pageSelector` helper also has a function to display a sitemap in a modal window.

```
$args = array(
'display_mode' => 'full'
);
$pageSelector->sitemap($args);
```

Note that the `sitemap()` function loads an element, which is automatically printed to the screen, so there is no need to echo or print the result.

2
Working with Blocks

In this chapter we will cover the following recipes:

- ▶ Creating a custom block type
- ▶ Using block controller callback functions
- ▶ Sending variables from the controller to the view
- ▶ Adding items to the page header and footer from the block controller
- ▶ Creating custom block templates
- ▶ Including JavaScript in block forms
- ▶ Including JavaScript in the block view
- ▶ Including CSS in the block view
- ▶ Loading a block type by its handle
- ▶ Adding a block to a page
- ▶ Getting the blocks from an area

Introduction

Blocks in concrete5 are small, modular pieces of visual presentation, which can add virtually any type of content to your website. Blocks can contain text content, HTML code, images, videos, an interactive map, or anything else you could think of. When you edit content on your concrete5 website, you are editing an instance of the content block type. Blocks get added to pages in special areas that get specified in theme layouts. concrete5 comes with a wide variety of different block types out of the box, and it is easy to create your own custom block types, enabling you to add unlimited potential to your website.

In this chapter, we will create a custom block type from scratch. This block type will just display some text that the user can edit through the **CMS** interface, and will serve as a basic "Hello World" example.

Creating a custom block type

Creating block types is a great way to add custom functionality to a website. This is the preferred way to add things like calendars, dealer locators, or any other type of content that is visible and repeatable on the frontend of the website.

Getting ready

The code for this recipe is available to download from the book's website for free. We are going to create a fully functioning block type that will display content on our website.

How to do it...

The steps for creating a custom block type are as follows:

1. First, you will need to create a directory in your website's root /blocks directory. The name of the directory should be underscored and will be used to refer to the block throughout the code. In this case, we will create a new directory called /hello_world.

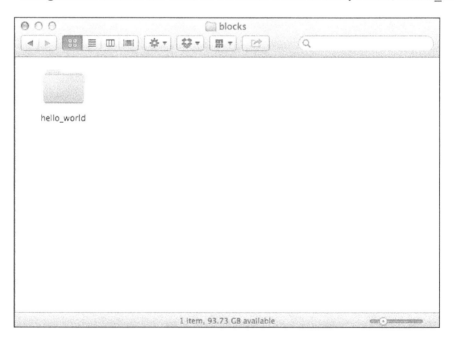

2. Once you have created the `hello_world` directory, you will need to create the following files:

   - `controller.php`
   - `db.xml`
   - `form.php`
   - `add.php`
   - `edit.php`
   - `view.php`
   - `view.css`

3. Now, we will add code to each of the files. First, we need to set up the `controller` file. The `controller` file is what powers the block. Since this is a very basic block, our controller only will contain information to tell concrete5 some details about our block, such as its name and description.

4. Add the following code to `controller.php`:

```php
class HelloWorldBlockController extends BlockController {
  protected $btTable = "btHelloWorld";
  protected $btInterfaceWidth = "300";
  protected $btInterfaceHeight = "300";
  public function getBlockTypeName() {
    return t('Hello World');
  }
  public function getBlockTypeDescription() {
    return t('A basic Hello World block type!');
  }
}
```

5. Notice that the class name is `HelloWorldBlockController`. concrete5 conventions dictate that you should name your block controllers with the same name as the `block` directory in camel case (for example: CamelCase) form, and followed by `BlockController`. The `btTable` class variable is important, as it tells concrete5 what database table should be used for this block. It is important that this table doesn't already exist in the database, so it's a good idea to give it a name of `bt` (short for "block type") plus the camel cased version of the block name.

6. Now that the controller is set up, we need to set up the `db.xml` file. This file is based off of the ADOXMLS format, which is documented at `http://phplens.com/lens/adodb/docs-datadict.htm#xmlschema`. This XML file will tell concrete5 which database tables and fields should be created for this new block type (and which tables and fields should get updated when your block type gets updated).

7. Add the following XML code to your `db.xml` file:

```xml
<?xml version="1.0"?>
<schema version="0.3">
  <table name="btHelloWorld">
    <field name="bID" type="I">
      <key />
      <unsigned />
    </field>
      <field name="title" type="C" size="255">
      <default value="" />
    </field>
      <field name="content" type="X2">
      <default value="" />
    </field>
  </table>
</schema>
```

8. concrete5 blocks typically have both an `add.php` and `edit.php` file, both of which often do the same thing: show the form containing the block's settings. Since we don't want to repeat code, we will enter our form HTML in a third file, `form.php`, and include that file in both `add.php` and `edit.php`.

```php
<?php
  $form = Loader::helper('form');
?>
<div>
  <label for="title">Title</label>
  <?php echo $form->text('title', $title); ?>
</div>
<div>
  <label for="content">Content</label>
  <?php echo $form->textarea('content', $content); ?>
</div>
```

9. Once that is all set, add this line of code to both `add.php` and `edit.php` to have this HTML code appear when users add and edit the block:

```php
<?php include('form.php') ?>
```

10. Add the following HTML to your `view.php` file:

```php
<h1><?php echo $title ?></h1>
<div class="content">
    <?php echo $content ?>
</div>
```

11. Finally, for a little visual appeal, add the following code to `view.css`:

```
content {
  background: #eee;
  padding: 20px;
  margin: 20px 0;
  border-radius: 10px;
}
```

12. Now all of the files have been filled with the code to make our Hello World block function. Now we need to install this block in concrete5 so we can add it to our pages.

13. To install the new block, you will need to sign into your concrete5 website and navigate to `/dashboard/blocks/types/`. If you happen to get a PHP fatal error here, clear your concrete5 cache by visiting `/dashboard/system/optimization/clear_cache` (it is always a good idea to disable the cache while developing in concrete5).

14. At the top of the **Block Types** screen, you should see your **Hello World** block, ready to install. Click on the **Install** button.

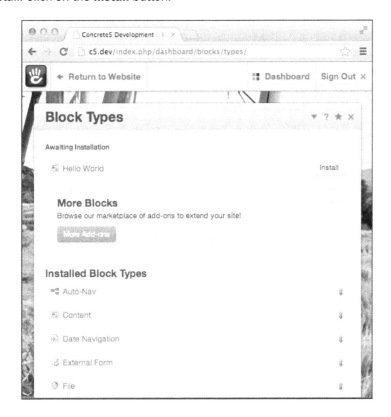

15. Now the block is installed and ready to add to your site!

How it works...

Let's go through the code that we just wrote, step-by-step.

In `controller.php`, there are a few protected variables at the top of the class. The `$btTable` variable tells concrete5 which table in the database holds the data for this block type. The `$btInterfaceWidth` and `$btInterfaceHeight` variables determine the initial size of the dialog window that appears when users add your block to a page on their site.

We put the block's description and name in special `getter` functions for one reason, to potentially support for translations down the road. It's best practice to wrap any strings that appear in concrete5 in the global `t()` function.

The `db.xml` file tells concrete5 what database tables should be created when this block gets installed. This file uses the ADOXMLS format to generate tables and fields. In this file, we are telling concrete5 to create a table called `btHelloWorld`. That table should contain three fields, an `ID` field, the `title` field, and the `content` field. The names of these fields should be noted, because concrete5 will require them to match up with the names of the fields in the HTML form.

In `form.php`, we are setting up the settings form that users will fill out to save the block's content. We are using the Form Helper to generate the HTML for the various fields. Notice how we are able to use the `$title` and `$content` variables without them being declared yet. concrete5 automatically exposes those variables to the form whenever the block is added or edited. We then include this form in the `add.php` and `edit.php` files.

The `view.php` file is a template file that contains the HTML that the end users will see on the website. We are just wrapping the title in an `<h1>` tag and the content in a `<div>` with a class of `.content`.

concrete5 will automatically include `view.css` (and `view.js`, if it happens to exist) if they are present in your block's directory. Also, if you include an `auto.js` file, it will automatically be included when the block is in edit mode. We added some basic styling to the `.content` class and concrete5 takes care of adding this CSS file to your site's `<head>` tag.

See also

- The *Sending variables from the controller to the view* recipe
- The *Adding items to the page header and footer from the block controller* recipe
- The *Including CSS in the block view* recipe
- The *Including JavaScript in the block view* recipe

Using block controller callback functions

The block controller class contains a couple of special functions that get automatically called at different points throughout the page load process. You can look into these callbacks to power different functionalities of your block type.

Getting ready

To get started, you will need a block type created and installed. See the previous recipe for a lesson on creating a custom block type. We will be adding some methods to `controller.php`.

How to do it...

The steps for using block controller callback functions are as follows:

1. Open your block's `controller.php` file.

2. Add a new function called `on_start()`:

   ```
   public function on_start() {
   }
   ```

3. Write a `die` statement that will get fired when the controller is loaded.

   ```
   die('hello world');
   ```

4. Refresh any page containing the block type. The page should stop rendering before it is complete with your debug message.

5. Be sure to remove the `die` statement, otherwise your block won't work anymore!

How it works...

concrete5 will call the various callback functions at different points during the page load process. The `on_start()` function is the first to get called. It is a good place to put things that you want to happen before the block is rendered.

The next function that gets called depends on how you are interacting with the block. If you are just viewing it on a page, the `view()` function gets called. If you are adding or editing the block, then the `add()` or `edit()` functions will get called as appropriate. These functions are a good place to send variables to the view, which we will show how to do in the next recipe. The `save()` and `delete()` functions also get called automatically at this point, if the block is performing either of those functions.

After that, concrete5 will call the `on_before_render()` function. This is a good time to add items to the page header and footer, since it is before concrete5 renders the HTML for the page. We will be doing this later on in the chapter.

Finally, the `on_page_view()` function is called. This is actually run once the page is being rendered, so it is the last place where you have the code executed in your block controller. This is helpful when adding HTML items to the page.

There's more...

The following functions can be added to your controller class and they will get called automatically at different points throughout the block's loading process.

- ▸ `on_start`
- ▸ `on_before_render`
- ▸ `view`
- ▸ `add`
- ▸ `edit`
- ▸ `on_page_view`
- ▸ `save`
- ▸ `delete`

For a complete list of the callback functions available, check out the source for the block controller library, located in `/concrete/core/libraries/block_controller.php`.

See also

- ▸ The *Sending variables from the controller to the view* recipe
- ▸ The *Adding items to the page header and footer from the block controller* recipe

Sending variables from the controller to the view

A common task in MVC programming is the concept of setting variables from a controller to a view. In concrete5, blocks follow the same principles. Fortunately, setting variables to the view is quite easy.

Getting ready

This recipe will use the block type that was created in the first recipe of this chapter. Feel free to adapt this code to work in any block controller, though.

How to do it...

In your block's controller, use the `set()` function of the `controller` class to send a variable and a value to the view. Note that the view doesn't necessarily have to be the `view.php` template of your block. You can send variables to `add.php` and `edit.php` as well. In this recipe, we will send a variable to `view.php`. The steps are as follows:

1. Open your block's `controller.php` file.

2. Add a function called `view()` if it doesn't already exist:

```
public function view() {
}
```

3. Set a variable called `name` to the view.

```
$this->set('name', 'John Doe');
```

4. Open `view.php` in your block's directory.

5. Output the value of the name variable.

```
<div class="content">
  <?php echo $name ?>
</div>
```

See also

▸ The *Using block controller callback functions* recipe

Adding items to the page header and footer from the block controller

An important part of block development is being able to add JavaScript and CSS files to the page in the appropriate places. Consider a block that is using a jQuery plugin to create a slideshow widget. You will need to include the plugin's JavaScript and CSS files in order for it to work.

In this recipe, we will add a CSS `<link>` tag to the page's `<head>` element, and a JavaScript `<script>` tag to bottom of the page (just before the closing `</body>` tag).

Getting ready

This recipe will continue working with the block that was created in the first recipe of this chapter. If you need to download a copy of that block, it is included with the code samples from this book's website.

This recipe also makes a reference to a CSS file and a JavaScript file. Those files are available for download in the code on this book's website as well.

How to do it...

The steps for adding items to the page header and footer from the block controller are as follows:

1. Open your block's `controller.php` file.

2. Create a CSS file in `/css` called `test.css`.

3. Set a rule to change the background color of the site to black.

   ```
   body {
      background: #000 !important;
   }
   ```

4. Create a JavaScript file in `/js` called `test.js`.

5. Create an alert message in the JavaScript file.

   ```
   alert('Hello!');
   ```

6. In `controller.php`, create a new function called `on_page_view()`.

   ```
   public function on_page_view() {
   }
   ```

7. Load the HTML helper:

   ```
   $html = Loader::helper('html');
   ```

8. Add a CSS file to the page header:

   ```
   $this->addHeaderItem($html->css('testing.css'));
   ```

9. Add a JavaScript file to the page footer:

   ```
   $this->addFooterItem($html->javascript('test.js'));
   ```

10. Visit a page on your site that contains this block. You should see your JavaScript alert as well as a black background.

How it works...

As mentioned in the *Using block controller callback function* recipe, the ideal place to add items to the header (the page's `<head>` tag) and footer (just before the closing `</body>` tag) is the `on_before_render()` callback function. The `addHeaderItem` and `addFooterItem` functions are used to place strings of text in those positions of the web document. Rather than type out `<script>` and `<link>` tags in our PHP, we will use the built-in HTML helper to generate those strings. The files should be located in the site's root `/css` and `/js` directories.

Since it is typically best practice for CSS files to get loaded first and for JavaScript files to get loaded last, we place each of those items in the areas of the page that make the most sense.

See also

▸ *Chapter 4, Using the Core Helpers*
▸ The *Using block controller callback functions* recipe

Creating custom block templates

All blocks come with a default view template, `view.php`. concrete5 also supports alternative templates, which users can enable through the concrete5 interface. You can also enable these alternative templates through your custom PHP code.

Getting ready

You will need a block type created and installed already. In this recipe, we are going to add a template to the block type that we created at the beginning of the chapter.

How to do it...

The steps for creating custom block templates are as follows:

1. Open your block's directory.
2. Create a new directory in your block's directory called `templates/`.
3. Create a file called `no_title.php` in `templates/`.
4. Add the following HTML code to `no_title.php`:

```
<div class="content">
  <?php echo $content ?>
</div>
```

5. Activate the template by visiting a page that contains this block.

6. Enter edit mode on the page and click on the block.

```
Click on "Custom Template".
```

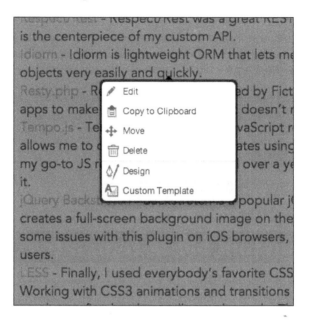

7. Choose "No Title" and save your changes.

There's more...

You can specify alternative templates right from the block controller, so you can automatically render a different template depending on certain settings, conditions, or just about anything you can think of. Simply use the `render()` function in a callback that gets called before the view is rendered.

```
public function view() {
    $this->render('templates/no_title');
}
```

This will use the `no_title.php` file instead of `view.php` to render the block. Notice that adding the `.php` file extension is not required. Just like the block's regular `view.php` file, developers can include `view.css` and `view.js` files in their template directories to have those files automatically included on the page.

See also

 ▸ The *Using block controller callback functions* recipe
 ▸ The *Creating a custom block type* recipe

Including JavaScript in block forms

When adding or editing blocks, it is often desired to include more advanced functionality in the form of client-side JavaScript. concrete5 makes it extremely easy to automatically add a JavaScript file to a block's editor form.

Getting ready

We will be working with the block that was created in the first recipe of this chapter. If you need to catch up, feel free to download the code from this book's website.

How to do it...

The steps for including JavaScript in block forms are as follows:

1. Open your block's directory.
2. Create a new file called `auto.js`.
3. Add a basic alert function to `auto.js`:
   ```
   alert('Hello!');
   ```
4. Visit a page that contains your block.
5. Enter edit mode and edit the block.
6. You should see your alert message appear as shown in the following screenshot:

How it works...

concrete5 automatically looks for the `auto.js` file when it enters add or edit mode on a block. Developers can use this to their advantage to contain special client-side functionality for the block's edit mode.

See also

- ▶ The *Including JavaScript in the block view* recipe
- ▶ The *Including CSS in the block view* recipe

Including JavaScript in the block view

In addition to being able to include JavaScript in the block's add and edit forms, developers can also automatically include a JavaScript file when the block is viewed on the frontend. In this recipe, we will create a simple JavaScript file that will create an alert whenever the block is viewed.

Getting ready

We will continue working with the block that was created in the first recipe of this chapter.

How to do it...

The steps for including JavaScript in the block view are as follows:

1. Open your block's directory.
2. Create a new file called `view.js`.
3. Add an alert to `view.js`:

   ```
   alert('This is the view!');
   ```

4. Visit the page containing your block.
5. You should see the new alert appear.

How it works...

Much like the `auto.js` file discussed in the previous recipe, concrete5 will automatically include the `view.js` file if it exists. This allows developers to easily embed jQuery plugins or other client-side logic into their blocks very easily.

See also

▸ The *Including JavaScript in block forms* recipe
▸ The *Including CSS in the block view* recipe

Including CSS in the block view

Developers and designers working on custom concrete5 block types can have a CSS file automatically included. In this recipe, we will automatically include a CSS file that will change our background to black.

Getting ready

We are still working with the block that was created earlier in the chapter. Please make sure that block exists, or adapt this recipe to suit your own concrete5 environment.

How to do it...

The steps for including CSS in the block view are as follows:

1. Open your block's directory.
2. Create a new file called `view.css`, if it doesn't exist.
3. Add a rule to change the background color of the site to black:

```
body {
    background: #000 !important;
}
```

4. Visit the page containing your block.
5. The background should now be black!

How it works...

Just like it does with JavaScript, concrete5 will automatically include `view.css` in the page's header if it exists in your block directory. This is a great way to save some time with styles that only apply to your block.

See also

- ▸ The *Including JavaScript in block forms* recipe
- ▸ The *Including JavaScript in the block view* recipe

Loading a block type by its handle

Block types are objects in concrete5 just like most things. This means that they have IDs in the database, as well as human-readable handles. In this recipe, we will load the instance of the block type that we created in the first recipe of this chapter.

Getting ready

We will need a place to run some arbitrary code. We will rely on `/config/site_post.php` once again to execute some random code. This recipe also assumes that a block with a handle of `hello_world` exists in your concrete5 site. Feel free to adjust that handle as needed.

How to do it...

The steps for loading a block type by its handle are as follows:

1. Open `/config/site_post.php` in your preferred code editor.
2. Define the handle of the block to load:

   ```
   $handle = 'hello_world';
   ```

3. Load the block by its handle:

   ```
   $block = BlockType::getByHandle($handle);
   ```

4. Dump the contents of the block to make sure it loaded correctly:

   ```
   print_r($block);
   exit;
   ```

How it works...

concrete5 will simply query the database for you when a handle is provided. It will then return a `BlockType` object that contains several methods and properties that can be useful in development.

Adding a block to a page

Users can use the intuitive concrete5 interface to add blocks to the various areas of pages on the website. You can also programmatically add blocks to pages using the concrete5 API.

Getting ready

The code in this chapter can be run anywhere that you would like to create a block. To keep things simple, we are going to use the `/config/site_post.php` file to run some arbitrary code.

This example assumes that a page with a path of `/about` exists on your concrete5 site. Feel free to create that page, or adapt this recipe to suit your needs. Also, this recipe assumes that `/about` has a content area called `content`. Again, adapt according to your own website's configuration.

We will be using the block that was created at the beginning of this chapter.

How to do it...

The steps for adding a block to a page are as follows:

1. Open `/config/site_post.php` in your code editor.

2. Load the page that you would like to add a block to:

   ```
   $page = Page::getByPath('/about');
   ```

3. Load the block by its handle:

   ```
   $block = BlockType::getByHandle('hello_world');
   ```

4. Define the data that will be sent to the block:

   ```
   $data = array(
     'title' => 'An Exciting Title',
     'content' => 'This is the content!'
   );
   ```

5. Add the block to the page's content area:

   ```
   $page->addBlock($block, 'content', $data);
   ```

How it works...

First you need to get the target page. In this recipe, we get it by its path, but you can use this function on any `Page` object. Next, we need to load the block type that we are adding. In this case, we are using the one that was created earlier in the chapter. The block type handle is the same as the directory name for the block.

We are using the `$data` variable to pass in the block's configuration options. If there are no options, you will need to pass in an empty array, as concrete5 does not allow that parameter to be blank. Finally, you will need to know the name of the content area; in this case, the content area is called "content".

See also

- ▶ The *Creating a custom block type* recipe
- ▶ The *Loading a block type by its handle* recipe
- ▶ The *Getting a page by its path* recipe in *Chapter 1, Pages and Page Types*

Getting the blocks from an area

concrete5 pages can have several different areas where blocks can be added. Developers can programmatically get an array of all of the block objects in an area. In this recipe, we will load a page and get a list of all of the blocks in its main content area.

Getting ready

We will be using `/config/site_post.php` to run some arbitrary code here. You can place this code wherever you find appropriate, though.

This example assumes the presence of a page with a path of `/about`, and with a content area called `content`. Make the necessary adjustments in the code as needed.

How to do it...

The steps for getting the blocks from an area are as follows:

1. Open `/config/site_post.php` in your code editor.
2. Load the page by its path:
   ```
   $page = Page::getByPath('/about');
   ```
3. Get the array of blocks in the page's content area.
   ```
   $blocks = $page->getBlocks('content');
   ```

4. Loop through the array, printing each block's handle.

```
foreach ($blocks as $block) {
  echo $block->getBlockTypeHandle().'<br />';
}
```

5. Exit the process.

```
exit;
```

How it works...

concrete5 will return an array of block objects for every block that is contained within a content area. Developers can then loop through this array to manipulate or read the block objects.

3
Files and File Sets

In this chapter, we will cover the following:

- ▶ Loading a file by its ID
- ▶ Getting a file's path
- ▶ Getting a list of files
- ▶ Uploading a file to the file manager
- ▶ Loading a file set by its ID
- ▶ Adding a file to a file set
- ▶ Removing a file from a file set
- ▶ Checking if a file is part of a file set
- ▶ Getting all of the files in a file set
- ▶ Duplicating a file
- ▶ Deleting a file
- ▶ Reindexing a file's search attributes
- ▶ Setting passwords on file objects
- ▶ Setting permissions on files
- ▶ Getting the download URL for a file
- ▶ Getting the download statistics for a file
- ▶ Adding a file picker to a form

Introduction

In addition to robust content editing features, **concrete5** comes with a powerful tool to manage static files on your website, called the **file manager**. The file manager is where you can store any type of static document, including images, videos, PDFs, documents, and audio files. The file manager allows you to create downloadable links to the files, embed photos into your site content, and much more. You can even assign permissions to files inside the file manager to allow for greater control in deciding what files users can download.

Working with files through the concrete5 interface is a delight, but sometimes you will want to integrate the powerful functionality of the file manager into your own custom applications built in concrete5. In this chapter, we will show how to interact with files, upload new files, and even upload new files to the file manager.

A note about the code in this chapter

Much of the code presented in this chapter can go just about anywhere in a concrete5 application. Since we are just going to be trying out simple code snippets, it makes sense to experiment with this code in a sandbox area. There are a few places in concrete5 that make sense for this, but we will be using /config/site_post.php to test out our code.

It is a good idea to erase any experimental and arbitrary code from site_post.php after each recipe, so that your site is ready for the next exercise.

Also, we will need to dump the contents of variables from time to time. Each PHP developer has his or her own way of doing this, but in this chapter we will be using a custom debug function. You may recognize this function from *Chapter 1, Pages and Page Types*. We will continue using it here, as it makes the output easy to read and saves some time while developing.

Place the following PHP function at the top of /config/site_post.php:

```
function my_debug($var) {
    echo '<pre>';
    print_r($var);
    echo '</pre>';
    exit;
}
```

Now we can dump variable contents by calling my_debug($variableName) and see a nicely formatted output of the contents of the variable. Feel free to use print_r or var_dump as an alternative.

Placing debug code in site_post.php is great for experimentation and trying out the concrete5 API, but it will disrupt the regular operation of a concrete5 website. It is recommended that all of the recipes in this chapter be performed on a testing copy of concrete5.

Loading a file by its ID

The most common interaction with files for most concrete5 developers is loading files and interacting with them. To do this, we must load a file by its ID. The code in this recipe can be placed wherever you need to load a file and retrieve or modify its attributes.

Getting ready

We will need to know the ID of the file that we are loading. In this recipe, we will load a file with the **ID** of `17`. If your concrete5 site does not have a file with an **ID** of `17`, upload a new file to the file manager and change the **ID** in this recipe to match the **ID** of the newly uploaded file. You can get the **ID** of a file by visiting the file manager, clicking on a file, and choosing **Properties**.

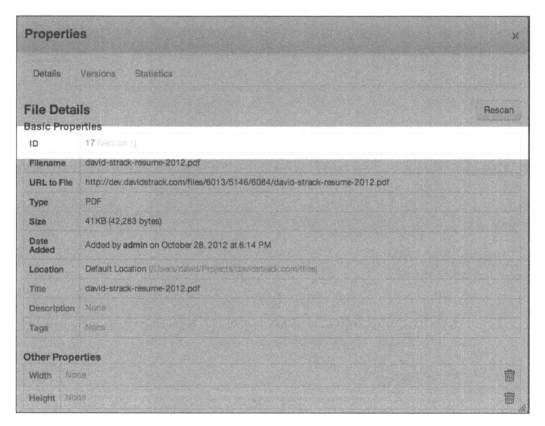

How to do it...

Have a look at the following steps:

1. Open `/config/site_post.php` in your code editor, or place this code, wherever it is appropriate in your own application.

2. Declare the ID of the file to load and be sure to set this to something relevant for your system:

   ```
   $fileId = 17;
   ```

3. Load the file:

   ```
   $file = File::getByID($fileId);
   ```

4. Dump the contents of the file variable:

   ```
   my_debug($file);
   ```

How it works...

concrete5 will use this function to load the relevant file from the database, based on the numeric ID that you passed in. The static `getByID` function will return a fully loaded `file` object that you can work further with.

Getting a file's path

Once you have loaded the `file` object, there are a multitude of different methods that you can call, to get all of the different attributes associated with that file. One of the most common and important attributes is that file's path.

Getting ready

In this recipe, we will get a file's path and use it to display an image stored in the file manager.

Once again, we will be referencing an image with the ID of `1`. Be sure to adapt the code in this recipe to load an image that actually exists in your concrete5 installation.

How to do it...

Have a look at the following steps:

1. Open `/config/site_post.php` in your editor.

2. Declare the ID of the file to be loaded:

   ```
   $fileId = 1;
   ```

3. Load the file by its ID:

```
$file = File::getByID($fileId);
```

4. Get the file's path:

```
$path = $file->getRelativePath();
```

5. Output the path to the screen:

```
echo $path;
exit;
```

How it works...

The file manager stores files in various locations through the concrete5 website, typically beneath the `files/` folder, which gets broken up into a few machine-readable folders consisting of integers. Since these paths are too hard to figure out and predict on a regular basis, the file object API allows us to get those paths with a simple function call.

There's more...

You will need the actual absolute path of a file, if you are working with the image in PHP's `fopen` function, for instance. For that, you will use the `getPath` function:

```
$fullPath = $file->getPath();
```

See also

▸   The *Loading a file by its ID* recipe

Getting a list of files

Many times, you will need to get several files at once. For example, if you were building a photo gallery, you would want to get a list of files to display in the gallery.

In this recipe, we will get a list of the first hundred images stored in the file manager and output their file paths.

Getting ready

This recipe assumes that there is at least one image stored in concrete5's file manager. Please make sure that your own version of concrete5 has one or more images stored.

How to do it...

1. Open `/config/site_post.php` in your preferred code editor.

2. Load the file list model:

   ```
   Loader::model('file_list');
   ```

3. Create a new instance of the `FileList` class:

   ```
   $list = new FileList();
   ```

4. Filter the list to only show images:

   ```
   $list->filterByType(FileType::T_IMAGE);
   ```

5. Get an array of images.

   ```
   $images = $list->get();
   ```

6. Loop through the images array and output each image's path.

   ```
   foreach ($images as $img) {
       echo $img->getRelativePath().'<br />';
   }
   exit;
   ```

How it works...

Much like listing pages and other object in concrete5, we loaded a `FileList` object that extends the core `DatabaseItemList` class. This afforded us an object-oriented manner in which to filter, search, and retrieve an array of files.

We called the `get()` function to return the images found in the file manager.

There's more...

concrete5 stores a few file type constants in the `FileType` class, which you can view in `concrete/libraries/file/types.php`. The following constants are available to filter by different file types:

- `FileType::T_APPLICATION`
- `FileType::T_AUDIO`
- `FileType::T_DOCUMENT`
- `FileType::T_IMAGE`
- `FileType::T_TEXT`
- `FileType::T_UNKNOWN`
- `FileType::T_VIDEO`

There are quite a few functions available on the `FileList` class to search and filter the list of files. The following are a few more functions that you can use:

▸ Filter the list by file extension (do not supply a period in the extension parameter):

```
$list->filterByExtension('mp3');
```

▸ Filter the list by a keyword phrase (searches by the file title, filename, and some other attributes):

```
$list->filterByKeywords('guacamole');
```

There are a few more specific filters available for the `FileList` class. You can dive into these filter functions by browsing the `FileList` class source code, or by viewing the online concrete5 developer documentation at `http://www.concrete5.org/documentation/developers/files/searching-and/`

See also

▸ The *Getting all of the files in a file set* recipe

Uploading a file to the file manager

Sometimes you will want to store user-supplied files in the file manager, or perhaps want to migrate the existing files on the server to the file manager. There are obvious security concerns whenever you are dealing with user-generated content, but there are plenty of legitimate reasons to want to programmatically add files to the file manager.

Getting ready

This recipe requires us to create a basic HTML form with a file upload input. We will place the HTML form in a single page located at `/single_pages/upload.php`. Be sure to install the single page by visiting `/dashboard/pages/single` and adding a new page with a path of `/upload`.

Since this recipe is a little bit more complex, it may be useful to check out the free code download for this chapter on this book's website.

We also will be using the custom debug function that we discussed in the chapter introduction.

How to do it...

Have a look at the following steps:

1. Create a new single page at `/single_pages/upload.php`.

2. Add the single page to the concrete5 website by visiting `/dashboard/pages/single` and entering the path `/upload`.

3. Create a basic HTML form in the `upload.php` file with a file input:

```
<form method="POST" enctype="multipart/form-data">
   File to upload: <input type="file" name="example_file"><br />
   <input type="hidden" name="file_upload" value="yes">
   <input type="submit" value="Upload!">
</form>
```

4. Create `/config/site_process.php`, if it does not exist.

5. In `site_process.php`, check to see if a file has been uploaded:

```
if ($_POST['file_upload'] == 'yes') {
}
```

6. Inside the `if` statement, load the `FileImporter` library:

```
Loader::library('file/importer');
```

7. Then, create a new instance of the `FileImporter` class:

```
$importer = new FileImporter();
```

8. Get the uploaded file from the `$_FILES` super global:

```
$file = $_FILES['example_file'];
```

9. Get the filename:

```
$name = $file['name'];
```

10. Get the file's current temporary location:

```
$path = $file['tmp_name'];
```

11. Add the file to the file manager:

```
$newFile = $importer->import($path, $name);
```

12. If `$newFile` is an integer, concrete5 has encountered an error. Output the error message:

```
if (is_numeric($newFile)) {
   die(FileImporter::getErrorMessage($newFile));
}
```

13. Otherwise, the file upload was successful.

14. Visit the site's file manager at `/dashboard/files/search/` to see the newly uploaded file.

How it works...

The `FileImporter` class takes the temporary path of the uploaded file (taken from the `$_FILES` super global) and a name for the file. The file is then added to the file manager, where it can be used throughout the concrete5 website.

See also

▶   The *Adding a file picker to a form* recipe

Loading a file set by its ID

concrete5 allows you to group files into sets. Some developers consider file sets to be similar to using folders on your computer, except that a file can be in multiple sets (or no sets) at a time, so a more apt description would be that, these are file categories.

File sets are great to organize files used for different purposes in your concrete5 website. For example, you might have one file set for a slideshow on the home page, while there is another file set for staff photos, and another for internal documents.

In this recipe, we will load a file set using its numeric ID.

Getting ready

In this section, we assume the existence of a file set with the ID of `1`. Please adjust the code in this recipe to suit your own concrete5 environment.

How to do it...

We will assume that we want to load a file set that has an ID of `1`. Have a look at the following steps:

1.   First, make sure you know the ID of the file set that you wish to load:

```
$id = 1;
```

2.   Load the file set:

```
$fileSet = FileSet::getByID($id);
```

3. If you wish, you can verify that the file set has loaded correctly by dumping the `$fileSet` variable:

```
my_debug($fileSet);
```

How it works...

concrete5 will query the database for the file set that has the ID you supplied. Once it finds the appropriate record, it will return a `FileSet` object that you can interact with.

There's more...

You can also retrieve file sets by providing their names as shown in the following code snippet:

```
$fileSet = FileSet::getByName('File Set Name');
```

See also

▸ The *Adding a file to a file set* recipe
▸ The *Getting a list of files* recipe

Adding a file to a file set

A useful aspect of working with file sets is the ability to add files to a given set using PHP code. Fortunately, this is a very simple task.

Getting ready

You will need to know the ID of the file that you are adding, or have the `File` object already loaded. This recipe will assume the existence of a file with the ID of 1 and of a file set also with an ID of 1.

How to do it...

Have a look at the following steps:

1. Open `/config/site_post.php` in your code editor.
2. Declare the file ID of the file that you wish to load.

```
$fileId = 1;
```

3. Declare the file set ID of the file set that you wish to load:

```
$fileSetId = 1;
```

4. Load the file by its ID:

```
$file = File::getByID($fileId);
```

5. Load the file set by its ID:

```
$fileSet = FileSet::getByID($fileSetId);
```

6. Add the file to the file set:

```
$fileSetFile = $fileSet->addFileToSet($file);
```

7. Dump the resulting FileSetFile object:

```
my_debug($fileSetFile);
```

How it works...

concrete5 will create an association between the file and the file set, and then return a `FileSetFile` object once it is complete.

There's more...

Alternatively, if you don't wish to load the file object, you can just provide the ID of the file that you are adding. Have a look at the following code snippet:

```
$fileSet = FileSet::getByID($filesetID);
$filesetFile = $fileSet->addFileToSet($fileId);
```

See also

▸ The *Removing a file from a file set* recipe
▸ The *Checking if a file is part of a file set* recipe

Removing a file from a file set

In addition to being able to add files to file sets, developers can also remove files from their file sets.

Getting ready

In this recipe, we will again assume the existence of a file with an ID of 1, as well as a file set with an ID of 1. Make sure to adjust the code as needed for your own concrete5 instance.

How to do it...

Have a look at the following steps:

1. Open `/config/site_post.php` in your code editor, so that we can play with some arbitrary code.

2. Declare the file ID:

   ```
   $fileId = 1;
   ```

3. Declare the file set ID:

   ```
   $fileSetId = 1;
   ```

4. Load the file by its ID:

   ```
   $file = File::getByID($fileId);
   ```

5. Load the file set by its ID:

   ```
   $fileSet = FileSet::getByID($fileSetId);
   ```

6. Remove the file from the file set:

   ```
   $fileSet->removeFileFromSet($file);
   ```

How it works...

concrete5 simply destroys the relationship between the file and the file set.

See also

▶ The *Adding a file to a file set* recipe
▶ The *Checking if a file is part of a file set* recipe

Checking if a file is part of a file set

Occasionally, developers may want to know if a file is a member of a certain file set. In this recipe, we will load a file, load a file set, and then find out if the file is a member of the given file set.

Getting ready

As usual, we will be assuming the existence of a file and a file set in this recipe. We will be using the ID of 1 for both the file and the file set, so be sure to make the necessary adjustments to the code to make this work in your own concrete5 system.

How to do it...

Have a look at the following steps:

1. Open `/config/site_post.php` and clear any existing code.
2. Declare the ID of the file to be loaded:

    ```
    $fileId = 1;
    ```

3. Declare the ID of the file set that we will be working with:

    ```
    $fileSetId = 1;
    ```

4. Load the file by its ID:

    ```
    $file = File::getByID($fileId);
    ```

5. Load the file set by its ID:

    ```
    $fileSet = FileSet::getByID($fileSetId);
    ```

6. If the file is a member of the file set, output a `yes` message:

    ```
    if ($file->inFileSet($fileSet)) {
        echo 'yes!';
    }
    ```

7. If the file is not a member of the set, output `no`:

    ```
    else {
        echo 'no';
    }
    ```

How it works...

concrete5 will do the heavy lifting of querying the database to find out if the file is a member of the given set.

See also

- ▸ The *Adding a file to a file set* recipe
- ▸ The *Removing a file from a file set* recipe

Getting all of the files in a file set

Now that we know how to load file sets and add files to them, we can learn how to get all of the files from a file set. We will be using the `FileList` class, which we first described earlier in this chapter.

Getting ready

We will continue working with the assumption that there is at least one file and one file set installed in concrete5, both with an ID of 1. Make the necessary adjustments to the variables in this recipe to suit your own needs.

How to do it...

Have a look at the following steps:

1. Open `/config/site_post.php` in your code editor, removing any existing code that might be in there.

2. Load the `FileList` model:

   ```
   Loader::model('file_list');
   ```

3. Create a new instance of the `FileList` model:

   ```
   $list = new FileList();
   ```

4. Declare the ID of the file set to filter by:

   ```
   $fileSetId = 1;
   ```

5. Load the file set:

   ```
   $fileSet = FileSet::getByID($fileSetId);
   ```

6. Filter the list by the loaded file set:

   ```
   $list->filterBySet($fileSet);
   ```

7. Get an array of files in the file set:

   ```
   $files = $list->get();
   ```

8. Loop through the array, printing each file's path to the screen:

   ```
   foreach ($files as $file) {
     echo $file->getRelativePath().'<br />';
   }
   exit;
   ```

9. Refresh your website to see the results.

How it works...

In this example, we are simply instantiating the `FileList` class, which will expose several methods to filter files. The method we are interested in is `filterBySet`.

We have to pass a `FileSet` object to this function and then we can call the `get` function, which will return an array of files that belong to that file set.

See also

- ▸ The *Getting a list of files* recipe
- ▸ The *Loading a file set by its ID* recipe

Duplicating a file

Just as in traditional file systems, concrete5 allows developers to duplicate files; in this recipe, we will load a file by its ID and then create a duplicate copy.

Getting ready

Be sure to adjust the file ID in this recipe to something that exists in your concrete5 database.

How to do it...

Have a look at the following steps:

1. Open `/config/site_post.php` in your preferred code editor.
2. Declare the ID of the file to be duplicated:

   ```
   $fileId = 1;
   ```

3. Load the file by its ID:

   ```
   $file = File::getByID($fileId);
   ```

4. Duplicate the file:

   ```
   $newFile = $file->duplicate();
   ```

5. Dump the contents of the new copy, using our custom debugging function that we created in the chapter intro:

   ```
   my_debug($newFile);
   ```

How it works...

concrete5 will create a carbon copy of the original file and return the new file once the function has completed.

Deleting a file

concrete5 allows developers to delete files through the PHP API. In this recipe, we will load a file by its ID and then delete it permanently.

Getting ready

Once a file has been deleted, it cannot be recovered. It is a good idea to experiment with a temporary or dummy file in this recipe so you do not delete anything important. This recipe will use the ID of 1 for the file to delete, but be sure to change this to something that you would be comfortable deleting.

How to do it...

Have a look at the following steps:

1. Open `/config/site_post.php` in your code editor.
2. Declare the ID of the file to delete:

    ```
    $fileId = 1;
    ```

3. Load the file by its ID:

    ```
    $file = File::getByID($fileId);
    ```

4. Delete the file:

    ```
    $file->delete();
    ```

How it works...

concrete5 will delete the file from your server's file system, as well as remove the reference to it in the MySQL database.

Reindexing a file's search attributes

When changing a file's attributes programmatically, sometimes the concrete5 search engine needs to be made aware of the new changes. In this exercise, we will reindex the search attributes for a file.

Getting ready

We will assume that a file with an ID of `1` exists in your concrete5 installation. Please adjust the ID in this recipe to a file that exists.

How to do it...

Have a look at the following steps:

1. Open `/config/site_post.php` in your code editor.
2. Declare the ID of the file to reindex:
   ```
   $fileId = 1;
   ```
3. Load the file by its ID:
   ```
   $file = File::getByID($fileId);
   ```
4. Reindex the search attributes:
   ```
   $file->reindex();
   ```

How it works...

concrete5 will query the database and update the search index for the given file. This will make sure that the internal search engine is able to find a file based on its most current attributes.

Setting passwords on file objects

concrete5 supports adding passwords to individual files, so site owners can restrict the download of these files to only those people who possess the shared password.

Getting ready

This recipe will continue with the assumption of a file with the ID of `1`. Please make sure to adjust this ID to match something that exists in your own concrete5 website.

How to do it...

Have a look at the following steps:

1. Open `/config/site_post.php` so we have a place to try out this code.
2. Declare the file ID:
   ```
   $fileId = 1;
   ```

3. Load the file by its ID:

```
$file = File::getByID($fileId);
```

4. Declare the password:

```
$password = 'secret';
```

5. Set the password on the file:

```
$file->setPassword($password);
```

How it works...

concrete5 will store the password in the database in plain text. Since this password is meant to be shared with several people, it is inherently insecure. As a result, concrete5 does not hash or encrypt the password for the file in the database. Once the password is set, the `on_file_set_password` event is fired.

There's more...

One can retrieve the password on a file by simply calling the `getPassword` function on the file:

```
$password = $file->getPassword();
```

See also

▶ The *Loading a file by its ID* recipe

Setting permissions on files

In the previous recipe, we discussed how to set a shared password on the file. Sometimes, though, more robust security is desired. For that, we can hook into the concrete5 permissions model to provide more advanced access control.

In this recipe, we will give a user read access to a file.

Getting ready

This example will assume the existence of a file with the ID of 1 and also of a user with an ID of 1. Adjust those IDs as needed.

How to do it...

Have a look at the following steps:

1. Open `/config/site_post.php` in your code editor.

2. Declare the ID of the file that we will be applying permissions to:

   ```
   $fileId = 1;
   ```

3. Load the file:

   ```
   $file = File::getByID($fileId);
   ```

4. Declare the ID of the user who will be receiving these permissions:

   ```
   $userId = 1;
   ```

5. Load the user:

   ```
   $user = UserInfo::getByID($userId);
   ```

6. Set the permissions on the file:

   ```
   $file->setPermissions($user, FilePermissions::PTYPE_MINE);
   ```

There's more...

concrete5 uses static constants for the permission modes (none, mine, and all). These constants are as follows:

▸ `FilePermissions::PTYPE_NONE`

▸ `FilePermissions::PTYPE_MINE`

▸ `FilePermissions::PTYPE_ALL`

See also

▸ *Chapter 7, Working With Users and Permissions*

Getting the download URL for a file

concrete5 can enforce permissions on files as well as keep track of download statistics by funneling all download requests through a special URL. This also has the added advantage of serving the correct HTTP headers to force the download to the user's computer.

Getting ready

As usual, we will have to assume the presence of a file with the ID of 1 in the file manager. Feel free to change this ID to something appropriate for your own website.

How to do it...

Have a look at the following steps:

1. Open `/config/site_post.php` in your favorite code editor.
2. Declare the ID of the file to load:

   ```
   $fileId = 1;
   ```

3. Load the file:

   ```
   $file = File::getByID($fileId);
   ```

4. Get the download URL:

   ```
   $url = $file->getDownloadURL();
   ```

5. Output the download URL to the screen:

   ```
   echo $url;
   exit;
   ```

How it works...

concrete5 passes the download request through a special URL that is able to track permissions, downloads, and also send the correct HTTP headers for the download.

See also

▶ The *Loading a file by its ID* recipe

Getting the download statistics for a file

If you serve files using the download function described in the previous recipe, then the download numbers would be stored in the database. You can get these statistics using just a few lines of code.

Getting ready

We will assume that a file with an ID of 1 exists in the file manager. Change this variable as needed for your own concrete5 website.

How to do it...

Have a look at the following steps:

1. Open `/config/site_post.php` in your preferred code editor.
2. Declare the ID of the file of which we want to get the statistics for:

    ```
    $fileId = 1;
    ```

3. Load the file:

    ```
    $file = File::getByID($fileId);
    ```

4. Get the statistics array:

    ```
    $stats = $file->getDownloadStatistics(false);
    ```

5. Dump the contents of the array:

    ```
    my_debug($stats);
    ```

How it works...

When we call the `getDownloadStatistics` method of the file object, concrete5 will return only the 20 most recent downloads by default. By providing `false` as the parameter, we are telling concrete5 to return all of the results.

Adding a file picker to a form

When building applications in concrete5, you will often find yourself creating **CRUD** (create, read, update, delete) interfaces on the dashboard for site editors and administrators to manage custom content. In some instances, you may have to handle file uploads on these backend forms. A useful tool on such forms would be to provide an interface to browse the file manager, rather than using the standard HTML file input. concrete5 uses the asset library widget to facilitate this for us.

Getting ready

In this recipe, we will create a basic HTML form that will send the selected file ID from the file manager along with the form submission. The full code for this recipe is available for download from the book's website.

How to do it...

Have a look at the following steps:

1. Create a new single page (if it doesn't already exist) at `/single_pages/upload.php`.

2. If you need to, add the single page to the sitemap, by visiting `/dashboard/pages/single` and entering `upload` as the page path.

3. In `upload.php`, load the asset Library helper:

   ```php
   <?php $assetLibrary = Loader::helper('concrete/asset_library'); ?>
   ```

4. Create an HTML form that outputs the file picker:

   ```html
   <form method="POST" enctype="multipart/form-data">
       <?php echo $assetLibrary->file('file_id', 'file_id', 'Select a file...') ?>
       <input type="hidden" name="file_upload" value="yes">
       <input type="submit" value="Upload the file!">
   </form>
   ```

5. Create `/config/site_process.php` if it doesn't already exist.

6. Check to see if a file upload has occurred:

   ```php
   if ($_POST['file_upload'] == 'yes') {
   }
   ```

7. Inside the `if` statement, get the file ID of the chosen file:

   ```php
   $fileId = $_POST['file_id'];
   ```

8. Output the chosen file ID to the screen:

   ```php
   echo 'You have chosen file #'.$fileId;
   exit;
   ```

How it works...

The asset Library helper will output all of the necessary HTML and JavaScript to provide a nice, modal interface for the user to select a file from the file manager (or upload a new file to the file manager). Once the user selects a file, the file ID will be added to a hidden input which has the name that you provided in the `file()` function's second parameter.

Once the user submits the form surrounding the file selector, the file ID will be included in the `$_POST` array (in this example, it would be in `$_POST['file_id']`), which you can then use for further storage or processing on the server side.

There's more...

You can also bring up a file manager window that is limited to only images. Use the following code to accomplish this:

```
<form action="save" method="POST">
  <p>Choose a file...</p>
  <?php
    $assetLibrary = Loader::helper('concrete/asset_library');
    $assetLibrary->image('file_id', 'file_id', 'Select a file...');
  ?>
</form>
```

You may notice that the only change here is that, instead of calling `file()` on the `asset library` class, we call `image()`. This will do the same exact thing as `file()`, except limit the modal window to contain only images.

See also

▸ The *Uploading a file to the file manager* recipe

4
Using the Core Helpers

In this chapter we will cover the following:

- ▶ Loading a helper class
- ▶ Using the Date helper
- ▶ Using the Encryption helper
- ▶ Loading an RSS feed with the Feed helper
- ▶ Managing files and directories with the File helper
- ▶ Creating custom forms with the Form helper
- ▶ Including a WYSIWYG editor on a form
- ▶ Generating HTML code with the HTML helper
- ▶ Generating and caching thumbnails with the Image helper
- ▶ Encoding and decoding JSON with the JSON helper
- ▶ Sending e-mails with the Mail helper
- ▶ Determining the MIME type of a file extension using the MIME helper
- ▶ Getting page URLs and breadcrumbs with the Navigation helper
- ▶ Working with strings using the Text helper
- ▶ Generating URLs with the URL helper
- ▶ Validating input data using the Validation helpers
- ▶ Preventing spam using the Captcha helper
- ▶ Getting a list of countries
- ▶ Getting a list of states and provinces
- ▶ Showing a color picker on a form
- ▶ Showing a date/time selector on a form

- ▸ Showing a rating widget on a form

- ▸ Using the banned words list

- ▸ Reading and writing to the system cache

- ▸ Writing to the debug log

- ▸ Reading and writing to the configuration registry

Introduction

During the course of developing custom applications within the concrete5 content management system, you will likely find yourself having to perform certain tasks multiple times. Tasks such as creating custom forms, sending e-mails, or parsing RSS feeds can all be sped up by utilizing the Core helper classes included with concrete5.

The concept of helpers in concrete5 might be familiar to developers who have previously worked with other popular MVC frameworks. Helpers are classes that provide miscellaneous, repeatable functionalities that can be used anywhere in your code. We will begin by showing how to load a helper class.

A note about the code in this chapter

As we've done in a few prior chapters, we will be making use of the /config/site_post. php file to run some arbitrary code. concrete5 doesn't have a great place to try out the API, so we will use site_post as our playground. Be sure to empty any experimental code before starting a new recipe, and perform all of these lessons on a development server.

We will continue using the custom debugging function that we created in *Chapter 1*, *Pages and Page Types*. Place the following function at the top of site_post.php if you'd like to follow along too:

```
function my_debug($var) {
    echo '<pre>';
    print_r($var);
    echo '</pre>';
    exit;
}
```

Of course, you're more than welcome to substitute our custom debugger with whatever you prefer.

Loading a helper class

The `Loader` class in concrete5 is useful for loading many different types of files in concrete5. We will use the `Loader` class to include and instantiate the Form helper.

How to do it...

1. Open `/config/site_post.php` in your code editor.

2. Make sure you know the "handle" of the helper that you wish to load. The handle is the name of the file that contains the helper class without the `.php` extension. As we want to load the Form helper, which exists at `/concrete/helpers/form.php`, the handle will be `form`:

   ```
   $handle = 'form';
   ```

3. Load the helper using the handle:

   ```
   $formHelper = Loader::helper($handle);
   ```

4. Let's double-check that the helper was loaded correctly by dumping the contents of the `$formHelper` variable:

   ```
   my_debug($formHelper);
   ```

How it works...

The `Loader` class includes PHP scripts, making it available for use. Also, when loading helpers, the included file will also be instantiated and returned, making it immediately available to use in your code.

There's more...

If you need to load a helper that is included in an add-on package, simply provide the package handle as a second parameter when loading the helper:

```
$helper = Loader::helper($handle, $packageHandle);
```

Using the Date helper

There are a number of date-related tasks that are simplified with the Date helper. We will look at a couple of ways to use the Date helper to assist in handling dates in your custom code.

Getting ready

In this recipe, we will explore a couple of the functions of the Date helper.

How to do it...

1. Open `/config/site_post.php` in your editor.

2. Load the Date helper:

   ```
   $date = Loader::helper('date');
   ```

3. Get the user's time:

   ```
   $userTime = $date->getLocalDateTime();
   ```

4. Get the system time:

   ```
   $systemTime = $date->getSystemDateTime();
   ```

5. Get an array of timezones:

   ```
   $timezones = $date->getTimezones();
   ```

6. Output each of these values to the screen:

   ```
   echo 'User time: ' . $userTime . '<br />';
   echo 'System time: ' . $systemTime . '<br />';
   my_debug($timezones);
   ```

How it works...

concrete5 wraps functions from both PHP and the Zend framework to create single-line tasks that would normally take several lines of code.

Using the Encryption helper

concrete5 makes it easy for developers to encrypt and decrypt strings using the included Encryption helper. In this recipe, we will use the Encryption helper to encrypt and decrypt some strings.

Getting ready

The majority of web servers come built-in with it, but it is important to make sure your web server has `mcrypt` installed as it is required for this helper to work.

How to do it...

1. Open `/config/site_post.php` in your code editor.

2. Load the helper:

```
$eh = Loader::helper('encryption');
```

3. Encrypt a basic string:

```
$encrypted = $eh->encrypt('hello');
```

4. Output the encrypted string:

```
echo $encrypted . '<br />';
```

5. Decrypt the encrypted string:

```
$decrypted = $eh->decrypt($encrypted);
```

6. Output the decrypted string:

```
echo $decrypted;
exit;
```

How it works...

The Encryption helper wraps the `mcrypt` PHP extension, and encodes the encrypted text in a Base64 encoded string.

See also

▸   The *Loading a helper class* recipe

Loading an RSS feed with the Feed helper

concrete5 comes with a third-party library called `SimplePie` that assists with parsing RSS feeds. The Feed helper wraps around the `SimplePie` library to provide a more convenient way to load RSS feeds.

How to do it...

1. Load the Feed helper:

```
$rss = Loader::helper('feed');
```

2. Define the URL of the RSS feed to load. We will load the news feed from Packt Publishing:

```
$url = 'http://www.packtpub.com/rss.xml';
```

3. Load the feed:

```
$feed = $rss->load($url);
```

4. Dump the contents of the feed object to verify that it loaded correctly:

```
my_debug($feed);
```

How it works...

The `load` function simply creates a new instance of the `SimplePie` class and loads the feed specified in the parameter. The `load` function then returns a `SimplePie` object based on the feed that was loaded.

There's more...

You can learn more about `SimplePie` and how to use the feed objects by visiting `http://simplepie.org`.

Managing files and directories with the File helper

Working with files and directories that exist on the web server can sometimes be a tedious task. The concrete5 File helper provides convenience methods to make working with files and directories a much simpler task.

Getting ready

This exercise will deal a lot with hypothetical files and filenames. This is meant more as an exploration of the File helper API, so feel free to substitute some of the filenames here for actual files that exist in your system.

How to do it...

1. Load the File helper:

```
$fh = Loader::helper('file');
```

2. Sanitize a filename so that it is suitable for saving:

```
$filename = 'Make This Eligible!';
$cleanName = $fh->sanitize($filename);
echo $cleanName; // outputs 'make_this_eligible'
```

3. Get the extension of a filename:

```
$ext = $fh->getExtension('image.png');
echo $ext; // outputs 'png'
```

4. Change the extension of a file:

```
$newFilename = $fh->replaceExtension('image.png', 'jpeg');
echo $newFilename; // outputs 'image.jpeg'
```

5. Get a file's contents:

```
$contents = $fh->getContents('data.txt');
```

6. Force a file to download to the user's computer:

```
$fh->forceDownload('/path/to/file.zip');
```

7. Copy a directory's contents to another directory:

```
$fh->copyAll('/source', '/target');
```

8. Delete all of the files in a directory:

```
$fh->removeAll('/directory/to/delete');
```

How it works...

The File helper makes use of many of the built-in functions of PHP, such as `file_get_contents`, `unlink`, and `copy`. The helper takes these functions several steps further by wrapping them with additional logic to make most of these operations only require a single line of code.

There's more...

There are some other functions that the File helper provides, which can be discovered by viewing the source code of the file in `concrete/core/helpers/file.php`.

See also

▸ The *Loading a helper class* recipe

Creating custom forms with the Form helper

Creating forms is one of the most common tasks that web developers are faced with on a regular basis. concrete5 provides the Form helper to make creating forms easy. In this recipe, we will create a feedback form using the Form helper.

Getting ready

The code in this recipe will be inserted into a `<form>` element on our website. See the complete example code on the website for this book. Our form will contain the following fields:

- **Name** (text input)
- **Email Address** (text input)
- **Reason for Contacting** (select box)
- **Message** (textarea)

How to do it...

1. Create a new single page by adding a new file located at `/single_pages/example_form.php`.

2. Install the single page by visiting `/dashboard/pages/single` on your concrete5 website. Enter `example_form` as the path for the new page.

3. Load the Form helper:
   ```
   $form = Loader::helper('form');
   ```

4. Output the field for the **Name** input:
   ```
   echo $form->text('name');
   ```

5. Output the field for the **Email Address** input:
   ```
   echo $form->email('email');
   ```

6. Create an associative array containing the options that will appear in the **Reason for Contacting** select box:
   ```
   $options = array(
       'general' => 'General Feedback',
       'support' => 'Technical Support',
       'return' => 'Returns / Refunds'
   );
   ```

7. Output the **Reason for Contacting** select box:
   ```
   echo $form->select('reason_for_contacting', $options);
   ```

8. Show the **Message** textarea:
   ```
   echo $form->textarea('message');
   ```

How it works...

The Form helper's functions return HTML that can be directly inserted into your forms on the website. If you provide an extra parameter to these functions, you can pre-fill the field's value with whatever you like (unless the value is present in the HTTP request parameters, which in that case concrete5 will fill the field with that value). There are many benefits to creating forms this way, and one can save a lot of time by following the simple conventions presented here.

There's more...

There are many form elements that can be generated using the Form helper. Radio buttons, checkboxes, select elements, text inputs, and more. Refer to the Form helper class at `concrete/core/helpers/form.php` or visit the concrete5 developer's documentation at `http://www.concrete5.org/documentation/developers/forms/`.

See also

▶ The *Loading a helper class* recipe

Including a WYSIWYG editor on a form

concrete5, being a content management system, comes with built-in **What You See Is What You Get** (**WYSIWYG**) editors, specifically, a popular open source editor called **TinyMCE**. Developers can include this editor in their custom HTML forms. In this recipe, we will add a WYSIWYG editor to the form that we created in the previous recipe.

Getting ready

We will be building upon the form that was created in the previous recipe. The free code download from this book's website will give you a good starting point if you need to catch up.

How to do it...

1. Open `/single_pages/example_form.php`.

2. At the top of the file, include the JavaScript element to initialize the editor:

    ```
    Loader::element('editor_init');
    ```

3. Below that, include the default TinyMCE configuration element:

    ```
    Loader::element('editor_config');
    ```

4. Above the existing textarea output, load the element containing the editor's controls:

    ```
    Loader::element('editor_controls');
    ```

5. Replace the existing textarea output with a new one:

```
echo $form->textarea('content', '', array('style' =>
'width:100%;', 'class' => 'ccm-advanced-editor'));
```

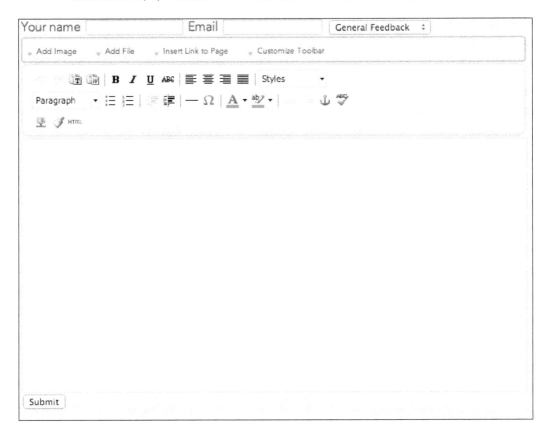

How it works...

The modified TinyMCE editor that concrete5 uses requires a lot of JavaScript to be in place before it can be included on a web page. concrete5 elements contain repeatable blocks of HTML, (or CSS and JavaScript in the form of `<style>` and `<script>` tags). At the top of our form, we include the elements with the TinyMCE JavaScript and the configuration settings.

It's optional, but it's a good idea to include the editor's control elements right above the textarea that will become the WYSIWYG editor. These controls have concrete5-specific functions, such as inserting links to pages in the site map or including images from the file manager. Note that as these controls mainly provide functionality relevant to site editors, these controls are better suited for backend forms, rather than use by end users.

Finally, we output a regular textarea element, but with a class of `ccm-advanced-editor`, which tells TinyMCE to turn this into a WYSIWYG editor.

See also

▶ The *Creating custom forms with the Form helper* recipe

Generating HTML code with the HTML helper

In many situations, you will want to avoid writing HTML strings in your PHP server-side code, as it can really clutter your code and make it harder to read. The HTML helper in concrete5 can help you avoid that by providing a nice, object oriented way to generate HTML code.

Getting ready

This recipe assumes that `/css/example.css`, `/js/example.js`, and `/images/icon.png` all exist on your site. You can perform this recipe without those files existing, concrete5 will simply output a path to those non-existent files.

How to do it...

1. Make the HTML helper available for use:

   ```
   $html = Loader::helper('html');
   ```

2. Output a CSS `<link>` tag, linking to a CSS file stored at `/css/example.css`:

   ```
   echo $html->css('example.css');
   ```

3. Output a JavaScript `<script>` tag, setting the `src` attribute to a file that exists at `/js/example.js`:

   ```
   echo $html->javascript('example.js');
   ```

4. Output an image `<img>` tag, showing an image that is stored at `/images/icon.png`:

   ```
   echo $html->image('icon.png');
   exit;
   ```

How it works...

concrete5 will recursively look through several directories to find the appropriate files that you need. It will then wrap the source path in the appropriate tag, whether it is a script, a CSS link, or an image.

See also

▶ The *Loading a helper class* recipe

Generating and caching thumbnails with the Image helper

Many types of applications make use of thumbnails to display representations of larger images. This allows users to see many images on one page without having to wait for several large file sizes of images to load.

Getting ready

The Image helper's thumbnail generator accepts a `File` object, so make sure to refer to *Chapter 3, Files and File Sets*, to know how to get those loaded.

How to do it...

1. Open `/config/site_post.php` in your code editor.

2. Load the Image helper:

    ```
    $ih = Loader::helper('image');
    ```

3. Load the `File` object that we want to create a thumbnail of. This should be an image (JPEG, PNG, or GIF) and should exist in the File Manager. We will use the ID of 1 for our example image:

    ```
    $fileId = 1;
    $image = File::getByID($fileId);
    ```

4. Generate a thumbnail with a height and width of 100 pixels, and crop the image to fit:

    ```
    $thumbnail = $ih->getThumbnail($image, 100, 100, true);
    ```

5. Echo the thumbnail image's source location:

    ```
    echo $thumbnail->src;
    exit;
    ```

How it works...

The Image helper will take the `File` object (or file path string) and first check to see if a thumbnail of that size has already been created. If it has, it will serve that thumbnail from the cache. If the thumbnail does not exist, concrete5 will use the `gd` PHP extension to resize and crop the image (if the fourth parameter is specified and set to `true`) and then save the new copy to the cache.

The helper returns a standard class object that has a few properties, `src`, `height`, and `width`. In this example, we are interested in the `src` property.

There's more...

You can have the Image helper applications output a thumbnail already wrapped in an `<img>` tag by simply calling the following:

```
echo $ih->outputThumbnail($image, 100, 100);
```

See also

▸ The *Loading a file by its ID* recipe in *Chapter 3, Files and File Sets*
▸ The *Loading a helper class* recipe

Encoding and decoding JSON with the JSON helper

Most PHP installations include handy JSON functions such as `encode_json` and `decode_json`, which allows developers to easily generate JSON data to pass through to the user's browser. concrete5 includes the JSON helpers to allow you to encode and decode JSON even on systems that do not have those functions available. This is particularly useful if you are developing an add-on that will run on several different types of environments.

How to do It...

1. Load the JSON helper:

   ```
   $json = Loader::helper('json');
   ```

2. Create an array that will be converted to a JSON string:

   ```
   $data = array(
       'name' => 'John Doe',
       'age' => '31'
   );
   ```

3. Encode the array into a JSON string:

```
$jsonStr = $json->encode($data);
```

4. Decode the JSON string back to an object:

```
$newObject = $json->decode($jsonStr);
```

How it works...

If the native JSON functions are present, these helper functions will simply wrap around those. On environments where the JSON encode and decode functions are unavailable, concrete5 will use a third-party JSON library to facilitate the encoding and decoding of the JSON strings.

See also

▸ The *Loading a helper class* recipe

Sending e-mails with the Mail helper

The ability to send e-mails from your web app can add a great layer of functionality to the end user. In this recipe, we will send an e-mail out with a simple subject and body.

How to do it...

1. Load the Mail helper:

```
$mail = Loader::helper('mail');
```

2. Specify the e-mail address that we wish to send the e-mail to:

```
$mail->to('test@example.com');
```

3. Specify the e-mail address that this e-mail is from (and who the recipient can reply to):

```
$mail->from('noreply@example.com');
```

4. Set the subject line of the e-mail:

```
$mail->setSubject('Hello from your concrete5 website!');
```

5. Set the message body:

```
$mail->setBody('This email was sent from your webserver!');
```

6. Send the e-mail:

```
$mail->sendMail();
```

How it works...

The Mail helper wraps around the `Zend_Mail` object, which is part of the Zend framework that concrete5 is built upon. The Mail helper will obey the concrete5 installation's settings, to send mails either by using PHP's built-in mail function, or by using an external SMTP server.

There's more...

You can send e-mails with templates, HTML text, and more with the Mail helper. Mail templates can be stored in the `/mail` directory of your concrete5 website. The following an example template that would exist at `/mail/test.php`:

```
$subject = 'Hello from your website!';
$body = 'This is the body! Hello, '.$name;
```

Notice how in this template, we refer to a variable called `$name`. To pass that variable into the template, call the `addParameter` function of the Mail helper:

```
$mail->addParameter('name', 'John Doe');
```

To load the template and apply extra parameters, call the `load` function just before sending. Remember that our template exists at `/mail/test.php`:

```
$mail->load('test');
```

See also

▶ The *Loading a helper class* recipe

Determining the MIME type of a file extension using the MIME helper

concrete5 can easily determine the **Multipurpose Internet Mail Extensions (MIME)** type of a file using the MIME helper.

How to do it...

1. Load the MIME helper:

   ```
   $mime = Loader::helper('mime');
   ```

2. Determine the MIME type of a JavaScript file:

   ```
   $jsMime = $mime->mimeFromExtension('js');
   ```

3. Verify that the MIME type is correct:

```
echo $jsMime; // outputs 'application/x-javascript'
exit;
```

How it works...

The MIME helper contains an array of several common MIME types and their related extensions. When you give the MIME helper an extension to find, it will simply find the related MIME type and return it to you.

There's more...

The MIME helper can also return the file extension of a given MIME type:

```
$jsExt = $mime->mimeToExtension('application/x-javascript');
echo $jsExt;
```

See also

▶ The *Loading a helper class* recipe

Getting page URLs and breadcrumbs with the Navigation helper

The Navigation helper can assist with two very important functions: getting accurate page URLs and generating a breadcrumb trail for a given `Page` object.

Getting ready

We will need to load a `Page` object and pass it to the Navigation helper, so make sure you are familiar with that.

How to do it...

1. Load the Navigation helper:

```
$nav = Loader::helper('navigation');
```

2. Load the `Page` object that we are going to work with. In this example, we will use a page located at `example.com/about-us`:

```
$page = Page::getByPath('/about-us');
```

3. Get the URL for the page:

```
$url = $nav->getCollectionURL($page);
```

4. Get an array of breadcrumb items (as `Page` objects) for the given page:

```
$breadcrumbs = $nav->getTrailToCollection($page);
```

How it works...

The Navigation helper checks your configuration settings and appends any base URLs or rewriting logic to the page's collection path. For breadcrumbs, the helper recursively travels up the sitemap from the given page to find all of the parent pages above it.

See also

▸ The *Loading a helper class* recipe

▸ The *Getting a Page object by its path* recipe in *Chapter 1, Pages and Page Types*

Working with strings using the Text helper

Another useful helper that concrete5 provides is the Text helper. The Text helper lets you perform several common (and sometimes complex) operations on strings with very little code.

How to do it...

1. Load the Text helper:

```
$text = Loader::helper('text');
```

2. Create a string to use for the example:

```
$str = 'This is a test';
```

3. CamelCase a string (CamelCase):

```
$camelCased = $text->camelcase($str);
echo $camelCased; // outputs "ThisIsATest"
```

4. Un-CamelCase that string:

```
$uncamelcased = $text->uncamelcase($camelCased);
echo $uncamelcased; // outputs 'this_is_a_test'
```

5. Create a URL-friendly string with hyphens:

```
$url = $text->urlify($str);
echo $url; // outputs 'this-is-a-test'
```

6. Create an underscored handle:

```
$handle = $text->handle($str);
echo $handle; // outputs 'this_is_a_test'
```

7. Remove all non-alphanumeric characters:

```
$alphaNum = $text->alphanum($str);
echo $alphaNum; // outputs 'This is a test'
Truncate a string and append an ellipsis at the end.
$trunc = $text->short$trunc = $text->short$trunc = $text->short
echo $trunc; // outputs 'This...'
exit;
```

How it works...

The Text helper wraps around several built-in PHP functions, as well as some third-party libraries to provide convenient, one-line functions that allow you to modify your text quickly and easily.

There's more...

The Text helper has a few other useful functions that are beyond the scope of this recipe, such as automatically creating links out of any URLs in a string or even automatically linking to Twitter handles. It is recommended that developers explore the source code of the Text helper to see some of the more niche functionality that it provides.

See also

▶ The *Loading a helper class* recipe

Generating URLs with the URL helper

The URL helper can generate URLs using some simple functions.

How to do it...

1. Load the URL helper:

```
$uh = Loader::helper('url');
```

2. Create an array that contains the URL parameters that we want to pass in. We will just make some stuff up for this example:

```
$params = array(
    'page' => '1',
    'filter' => 'events'
);
```

3. Build the URL:

```
$url = $uh->buildQuery('http://example.com', $params);
```

4. Output the URL to see the result:

```
echo $url; // outputs http://example.com?page=1&filter=events
exit;
```

How it works...

This function makes use of PHP's `http_build_query` function that can generate valid URLs when given an array of parameters.

There's more...

The URL helper also has a function to create a shortened URL using the TinyURL service.

```
$short = $uh->shortenURL('http://example.com');
echo $short; // outputs http://tinyurl.com/123abc
```

See also

▶ The *Loading a helper class* recipe

Validating input data using the Validation helpers

When building an application that accepts user data, it is definitely a good idea to make sure that users are filling out all of the required fields on a form.

Getting ready

Consider a comment form that has the following fields: Name, Email, Website, and Comment content. The name, e-mail, and content fields are required, but the website field is optional. We will use the Validation helper to determine if the user filled out all of the required fields.

How to do it...

1. Load the Validation helper:

```
$val = Loader::helper('validation/form');
```

2. Let's create an array to simulate the data that would be contained in the POST request (via the $_POST super global). We will intentionally leave email blank to see how the Validation helper behaves when a test fails:

```
$data = array(
    'name' => 'Jane Doe',
    'email' => '',
    'website' => 'http://example.com',
    'content' => 'Great post!'
);
```

3. Pass the array to the Validation helper so that it knows what to validate against:

```
$val->setData($data);
```

4. Specify the fields that are required, with error messages for each one:

```
$val->addRequired('name', 'Please enter a name.');
$val->addRequiredEmail('email', 'Please enter an email address.');
$val->addRequired('content', 'Please enter some content.');
```

5. Test the array to see if it passes the requirements.

```
$passed = $val->test();
Output the list of errors so the user knows what fields are
missing.
  if ($passed === false) {
    foreach ($val->getError()->getList() as $error) {
       echo $error . '<br />';
    }
  }
exit;
```

How it works...

The Validation helper is pretty basic in terms of functionality, it essentially checks for the presence of a given variable in the data array, and makes sure that it has some sort of value. Notice the use of addRequiredEmail in step 4. This function makes sure the e-mail address is present and also verifies that it is a proper e-mail address (not just any string).

The getError function on the Validation helper returns a ValidationErrorHelper object that has a function called getList that can provide an easy-to-use array of error messages.

There's more...

In addition to testing for regular strings and e-mails, you can also test for integer values:

```
$val->addRequiredInteger('age', 'Please enter your age.');
```

See also

▸ The *Loading a helper class* recipe

Preventing spam using the Captcha helper

As most web developers who have ever published a form online know, spam is an annoying and potentially damaging issue for site owners. concrete5 can help mitigate this problem with a built-in Captcha helper that can verify that form submissions are coming from humans, rather than automated scripts.

Getting ready

This recipe will explain how to use the Captcha helper. Typically, you will use this helper in the HTML views that your end-user would see (single page views, block views, and so on). An example of this helper in the context of a single page is included in the book's code download.

How to do it...

1. Load the Captcha helper:

   ```
   $captcha = Loader::helper('validation/captcha');
   ```

2. At the bottom of your form, display the CAPTCHA image and the input to allow the user to solve it:

   ```
   <?php echo $captcha->display(); ?> <br />
   <?php echo $captcha->showInput(); ?>
   ```

3. In the server-side code that processes the form submission, verify that the CAPTCHA was solved correctly:

   ```
   if ($captcha->check()) {
       // User passed, continue processing.
   }
   ```

How it works...

The Captcha helper takes advantage of a third-party library called `SecureImage` to generate the CAPTCHA images and related logic. If the user types the word in the image correctly, the `check` function will return `true`, and you can continue processing the form submission.

See also

▶ The *Loading a helper class* recipe

Getting a list of countries

Many times, web developers find themselves needing to provide a list of countries to users. Rather than hunt down this data or even manually assemble the data, concrete5 provides a helper to generate a list of all of the countries of the world. In this recipe, we will take the country list and create a `<select>` element that can be placed in a form, allowing users to select a country.

How to do it...

1. Create a single page at `/single_pages/example_form.php`.
2. Install the single page by visiting `/dashboard/pages/single` and typing `example_form` in the path input.
3. Open `/single_pages/example_form.php` in your code editor.
4. At the top of the file, load the country list helper:

   ```
   $list = Loader::helper('lists/countries');
   ```

5. Get the array of the available countries:

   ```
   $countries = $list->getCountries();
   ```

6. Load the Form helper:

   ```
   $form = Loader::helper('form');
   ```

7. Create an HTML form that contains a select element with all of the countries:

   ```
   <form>
       <?php echo $form->select('country', $countries); ?>
   </form>
   ```

How it works...

concrete5 takes the heavy lifting of assembling and maintaining a list of countries and builds it into the core list helper. The country's two-character code is provided as the array key, and the full name string as the value.

See also

▸ The *Loading a helper class* recipe
▸ The *Creating custom forms with the Form helper* recipe

Getting a list of states and provinces

In addition to providing lists of countries, concrete5 can also provide lists of states, provinces, and counties, for the countries in which such a list is applicable.

In this recipe, we will get a list of all of the counties of the United Kingdom and present them in a <select> input.

How to do it...

1. If it doesn't exist, create a single page at /single_pages/example_form.php.

2. Load the List helper:

```
$list = Loader::helper('lists/states_provinces');
```

3. Get the list of counties in the UK:

```
$counties = $list->getStateProvinceArray('UK');
```

4. Load the Form helper:

```
$form = Loader::helper('form');
```

5. Create an HTML form that has a <select> element containing the list of counties:

```
<form>
    <?php echo $form->select('county', $counties); ?>
</form>
```

How it works...

The state/province List helper works much like the Country helper, in that the concrete5 team has assembled a list of states/counties/provinces for various counties that can be accessed by providing the two-character code.

There's more...

If you want to get all of the states and provinces stored in the helper, you can use the following code:

```
$allProvinces = $list->getAll();
```

See also

- ▸ The c*Loading a helper class* recipe
- ▸ The *Creating custom forms with the Form helper* recipe

Showing a color picker on a form

concrete5 provides helpers to generate standard HTML form elements, but what about applications that need to allow users to pick a color? For those applications, concrete5 includes a color picker helper as well!

Getting ready

The color picker relies on jQuery UI, which isn't automatically included in concrete5, unless you are logged in as an administrator. Be sure to include jQuery UI's JavaScript and CSS files on the page if you use the color picker on the frontend of the site.

How to do it...

1. If it doesn't already exist, create a single page at `/single_pages/example_form.php`.
2. Install this single page on the dashboard if need be.
3. Load the color picker helper at the top of the file:

    ```
    $color = Loader::helper('form/color');
    ```

4. Output the color picker widget in an HTML form element:

    ```
    <form>
        <?php echo $color->output('color', 'Choose a color...') ?>
    </form>
    ```

How it works...

concrete5 will generate the HTML and JavaScript necessary to provide an interactive color picker widget. The first parameter passed to the `output` function is the name of the field, which is how the value will be accessed once the form is submitted. The second parameter is the text that will appear in a `<label>` element next to the color picker.

See also

▶   The *Loading a helper class* recipe

Showing a date/time selector on a form

A very common user experience when using web apps that require date inputs is to have the users choose the date on an interactive calendar, rather than typing the full date. concrete5 provides a helper to generate such widgets with ease. In this recipe, we will generate a date picker that will show a mini-calendar to allow users to choose a date.

Getting ready

concrete5 only automatically includes the JavaScript files for jQuery UI when users are logged in as administrators. If you wish to use the date picker in areas of the site where non-administrators can use it, be sure to include the jQuery UI JavaScript and CSS files in the page.

How to do it...

1.   Create a single page at `/single_pages/example_form.php` if it doesn't already exist.

2.   Be sure to install the single page on the dashboard by visiting `/dashboard/pages/single`.

3.   Load the date/time helper:

```
$datePicker = Loader::helper('form/date_time');
```

4.   Output the date picker into an HTML form:

```
<form>
   <?php echo $datePicker->date('date') ?>
</form>
```

How it works...

concrete5 makes use of the jQuery UI library to generate the JavaScript and CSS necessary to create an interactive date picker. The date/time helper generates all of the necessary boilerplate HTML and JavaScript, which makes using date pickers a very simple process.

There's more...

Sometimes developers will need to provide users with an interface to also select a time to go along with the date. This is simply a matter of calling a different function on the date/time helper:

```
echo $datePicker->datetime('date')
```

See also

▸ The *Loading a helper class* recipe

Showing a rating widget on a form

Modern web applications provide a set of star icons for users to click on, providing a "rating" of a given item. It is simple to include these types of UI components in concrete5 applications using the Rating helper.

How to do it...

1. Create a single page at `/single_pages/example_form.php` if it does not exist.
2. Install the single page by visiting `/dashboard/pages/single` and entering `example_form` as the page location.
3. Load the Rating form helper:

   ```
   $rh = Loader::helper('form/rating');
   ```

4. Output the rating widget:

   ```
   <form>
       <?php echo $rh->rating('rating', 60) ?>
   </form>
   ```

How it works...

The Rating helper makes use of a third-party jQuery plugin to provide an interactive rating chooser. The helper will take care of generating all HTML and JavaScript required to use this widget.

The output function requires two parameters: the name of the input and the initial value (an integer that is either 20, 40, 60, 80, or 100).

There's more...

If you'd like to just simply provide a read-only way to display a rating, the Rating helper can do that:

```
$rating = Loader::helper('rating');
$rating->outputDisplay(84);
```

Simply call the `outputDisplay` method and provide a value between 0 and 100.

See also

▸ The *Loading a helper class* recipe

Using the banned words list

concrete5 comes bundled with a list of profane and inappropriate English words that site owners can use to remove inappropriate content from their website. In this example, we will check a word to see if it is in the banned words list.

How to do it...

1. Load the banned words helper:

    ```
    $bannedWords = Loader::helper('validation/banned_words');
    ```

2. Check a word to see if it is in the banned words list:

    ```
    $isBanned = $bannedWords->isBannedWord('friendly');
    ```

3. If the word is in the banned words list, then `$isBanned` will be equal to `true`:

    ```
    var_dump($isBanned);
    exit;
    ```

How it works...

concrete5 checks the list of banned words (stored at `/concrete/config/banned_words.txt`) to see if it contains the word provided in the parameter.

There's more...

Site owners can customize and edit the banned words list by copying it to `/config/banned_words.txt` and adding or removing entries there.

See also

▶ The *Loading a helper class* recipe

Reading and writing to the system cache

Responsible developers will take extra steps to make sure their application is optimized for maximum performance. concrete5 has a built-in cache API that developers can hook into to cache their own custom data and improve performance, especially on large database lookups.

Getting ready

We will load a large amount of rows from the database (something that can impact performance in a negative way), and then store the resulting array in the cache to prevent future, resource-heavy data calls. This recipe will load from a hypothetical table called `Customers` that contains thousands of rows.

How to do it...

1. Load a large set of records from the database that will tax the server's resources. We will use a hypothetical table called `Customers`:

```
$db = Loader::db();
$customers = $db->getAll('SELECT * FROM Customers');
```

2. Store the results in the system cache:

```
Cache::set('customerList', false, $customers);
```

3. Read the results from the cache, preventing another intense database query:

```
$cachedCustomers = Cache::get('customerList', false);
```

How it works...

concrete5's cache library is a custom implementation of the `Zend_Cache` library, which comes with the Zend framework, upon which concrete5 is built. Calling the `set` function, you will specify the type of item that you are saving (in this case, we call it `customerList`), and an ID of the item we are saving (this is useful if you are saving several different objects of the same type—in this case we are not, so we just set this variable to `false`).

There's more...

You can delete an item that you have saved in the cache by sending in the type and the ID of the item that was stored. To delete our preceding customer list, you would write the following:

```
Cache::delete('customerList', false);
```

You can also flush the entire cache, removing all of the items that are stored inside:

```
Cache::flush();
```

See also

- The *Loading a helper class* recipe
- The *Loading the database object* recipe in *Chapter 5, Working with Databases and Models*
- The *Retrieving data from the database* recipe in *Chapter 5, Working with Databases and Models*

Writing to the debug log

Logging is a common practice in application development, but sometimes you might want to separate errors in your concrete5 app from errors that are specific to PHP or Apache. For this, you can write to concrete5's internal log that can be viewed from the dashboard by site administrators. In this recipe, we will simply write a couple of basic strings to the site's internal log.

How to do it...

1. Come up with the message string that you would like to write to the log:

```
$message = 'Hello, log!';
```

2. Write the message to the log:

```
Log::addEntry($message);
```

Reading and writing to the configuration registry

Storing key and value pairs in data dictionaries is a common task in any modern programming language. concrete5 allows you to store configuration settings using the `Config` class, rather than storing key/value settings in the database or elsewhere. In this recipe, we will write a configuration preference that signifies if the site administrator wants to allow comments on the site or not.

How to do it...

1. Write the preference to the system configuration dictionary:

   ```
   Config::save('allow_comments', true);
   ```

2. Read the value of the preference item:

   ```
   $allowComments = Config::get('allow_comments');
   ```

How it works...

concrete5 stores the key and value pairs in the `Config` table of the database. The `Config` class presents a clean and simple API to make writing and reading configuration values as easy as possible. These configuration keys persist throughout concrete5, so developers should take extra caution to prevent clashes with other configuration values of the same name. It's a good idea to prefix configuration keys with something unique to your own code, such as `cookbook_allow_comments`, in this case.

5
Working with
Databases and Models

In this chapter, we will cover the following:

- ▶ Configuring database credentials
- ▶ Loading the database object
- ▶ Retrieving data from the database
- ▶ Writing data to the database
- ▶ Guarding against SQL injections with prepared statements
- ▶ Creating a custom model class
- ▶ Reading from the database with active record
- ▶ Writing to the database with active record
- ▶ Updating a database record with active record
- ▶ Searching the database using active record
- ▶ Deleting objects using active record and model classes
- ▶ Defining relationships with active record

Introduction

Web applications get a great deal of their capabilities from being connected to a database. concrete5 is a **LAMP** application (runs on Linux, Apache, MySQL, and PHP). MySQL is the database that concrete5 uses, which is the most popular open source database in the world.

In this chapter, we will discover the ways to interact with the database in concrete5, both with plain SQL queries, and with the more object-oriented active record approach. We will learn how to safeguard against SQL injection attacks, create custom model classes, and query the database using objects and active record.

This chapter will use some basic SQL queries, so some familiarity with writing database queries is recommended.

Configuring database credentials

Before we are able to read and write to the database, we need to make sure concrete5 has the correct database credentials. Typically these credentials are set during installation, but if you are moving a concrete5 to another server or changing the username or password of the concrete5 user, it is important to know how to configure database access.

In this recipe, we will act as though we are specifying the credentials from scratch. This will allow us to explore each value that is stored in the database.

How to do it...

Have a look at the following steps:

1. Open `/config/site.php` in your preferred code editor.
2. Specify the host name of the database server. In many instances, this is simply `localhost`:

   ```
   define('DB_SERVER', 'localhost');
   ```

3. Set the username that concrete5 will use to connect to the database:

   ```
   define('DB_USERNAME', 'user');
   ```

4. Set the password for that users:

   ```
   define('DB_PASSWORD', 'password');
   ```

5. Finally, specify the name of the database that concrete5 will connect to:

   ```
   define('DB_DATABASE', 'concrete5');
   ```

How it works...

The `site.php` file is automatically loaded by concrete5 when the site is accessed. Developers can define configuration constants here using PHP's `define` function. The first parameter of the `define` function is the constant's name, do *not* change this. The second parameter, however, should contain the corresponding value for the particular setting.

Make sure that the user that you choose for concrete5 has sufficient access to the database and is allowed to perform all of the necessary queries.

Improperly configured database settings in this file will result in the website displaying an error.

Loading the database object

At the heart of performing queries on the database in concrete5, is the database object. The database object exposes several methods that allow developers to perform queries on the database.

How to do it...

Have a look at the following steps:

1. We will need a place to play around with some test code. Open `/config/site_post.php` which will serve us well in your code editor.

2. Write the following code snippet to load the database object:

    ```
    $db = Loader::db();
    ```

3. Now that the database object is loaded, take a look at some of the methods that it exposes:

    ```
    $methods = get_class_methods($db);
    ```

4. Dump the array of methods to the screen:

    ```
    var_dump($methods);
    exit;
    ```

How it works...

concrete5 will use the database settings from your configuration file (likely located at `/config/site.php`) and connect to the database, returning an object containing several useful methods for interacting with the database.

There's more...

If you'd like to connect to a database other than the one specified in `site.php`, you can pass in the new database credentials as parameters to the database loader, as shown in the following:

```
$db = Loader::db('host', 'user', 'password', 'database');
```

Retrieving data from the database

Once you have loaded the database object, you can perform queries against it. In this recipe, we will select the contents of the Users table, and echo out each username.

Getting ready

Make sure you understand how to write database queries with SQL before diving into writing queries by hand in concrete5. There are dozens of MySQL resources available online and in print that go far beyond the scope of this book!

How to do it...

Have a look at the following steps:

1. Load the database object:

   ```
   $db = Loader::db();
   ```

2. Write the query to select from the Users table:

   ```
   $query = 'SELECT * FROM Users';
   ```

3. Execute the query:

   ```
   $results = $db->getAll($query);
   ```

4. Loop through the results and echo each user's username:

   ```
   foreach ($results as $user) {
       echo $user['uName'].'<br />';
   }
     exit;
   ```

How it works...

This function works as you'd expect, but it takes a little of the tedium out of performing raw database queries with PHP and MySQL. Calling getAll function on the database object returns an array of all of the results. Each result is also an array, with keys that correspond to each column in the row.

There's more...

If you are performing a query where you are only selecting one column and expect one result (for instance, a COUNT query) you can use the getOne method to get the exact value that you need as shown in the following code snippet:

```
$count = $db->getOne('SELECT COUNT(*) FROM Users');
```

See also

▶ The *Writing data to the database* recipe

Writing data to the database

Of course, the majority of queries that can be performed on a MySQL database don't return any data. What if a developer needs to insert a row into a table? For that, we can use the execute method of the database object.

In this recipe, we will insert a new row into a table called CustomTable.

Getting ready

We will want to insert some rows to the database here, but we don't want to mess anything up in the normal concrete5 database tables. Create a dummy table to run some queries on by executing the following statement on your MySQL database (this SQL file is also included with the free code download from this book's website):

```
CREATE TABLE `CustomTable` (
    `id` int(11) unsigned NOT NULL AUTO_INCREMENT,
    `name` varchar(255) DEFAULT NULL,
    `country` varchar(255) DEFAULT '',
    PRIMARY KEY (`id`)
);
```

How to do it...

Have a look at the following steps:

1. Open /config/site_post.php in your code editor.
2. Load the database object:
   ```
   $db = Loader::db();
   ```

3. Write the `INSERT` query:

    ```
    $query = 'INSERT INTO CustomTable (name, country) VALUES ("John
    Doe", "US")';
    ```

4. Execute the `INSERT` query:

    ```
    $db->execute($query);
    ```

5. Output a success message, so that you know the update worked:

    ```
    echo 'done!';
    exit;
    ```

How it works...

The `execute` function allows a developer to run, literally, any query that the user has permission to run. In this case, we are simply executing a statement to add a new row to a custom table.

There's more...

The `execute` function can be used to run any arbitrary query on the database. For example, if we want to `TRUNCATE` (empty) the contents of `CustomTable`, we could write the following code snippet:

```
$query = 'TRUNCATE CustomTable';
$db->execute($query);
```

Guarding against SQL injections using prepared statements

A major source of security headaches in web applications has been SQL injection attacks. **SQL injections** can occur when user-supplied data is not properly escaped and sanitized before being inserted into an SQL command. Malicious users could use this as an opportunity to run arbitrary commands on the database, either exposing sensitive data, or performing destructive actions such as altering or removing data.

Fortunately, this is an easy problem to solve. Indeed, one could manually sanitize all user input before concatenating those inputs into SQL queries, but that is tedious and prone to human error (forgetting to sanitize one portion of the application could still leave it vulnerable to attack). The preferred way to guard against SQL injection is to use prepared statements.

Prepared statements (or parameterized statements) are just like regular SQL queries. The only difference is, instead of directly inserting the user-supplied parameters into the query, the database will run the base query and the parameter portions at separate times. Therefore, prepared statements will not be vulnerable to SQL injections.

When running queries that contain user-supplied data, it is important to use only prepared statements.

The database object in concrete5 supports prepared statements, and in this recipe, we will create a prepared statement which allow guests to search the Users table by username and get that user's email address in return.

Getting ready

This recipe will assume that your concrete5 system has a user with the username of admin. Feel free to adjust this code to make it suit your environment.

How to do it...

Have a look at the following steps:

1. Open /config/site_post.php in your code editor.

2. Load the database object:

   ```
   $db = Loader::db();
   ```

3. Create our prepared statement:

   ```
   $query = 'SELECT * FROM Users WHERE uName = ?';
   ```

4. Store the value that the user provided on an HTML form. We will pretend it was equal to admin:

   ```
   $username = 'admin';
   ```

5. Run the prepared query, with the statement as the first parameter, and the filter value as the second:

   ```
   $results = $db->getAll($query, $db->getAll($query, $db-
   >getAll($query, $db->getAll($query, $db->getAll($query,
   ```

6. Loop through the results and echo out each user's email address (there should be only one):

   ```
   foreach ($results as $user) {
       echo $user['uEmail'] . '<br />';
   }
   exit;
   ```

How it works...

Prepared statements are a feature of the database management system, in this case, MySQL. The database object in concrete5 utilizes this native feature to make it easy to use in a single-line function. This is because the query is prepared and executed before the parameters are applied; there is no risk of SQL injection. In addition to the security benefits, prepared statements are a great way to improve the performance on queries that are run several times.

There's more...

The database object supports executing prepared statements with more than one parameter. In these instances, simply provide the parameters in an array, with each value in the same order that it is specified in the query. Have a look at the following code snippet:

```
$sql = 'INSERT INTO CustomTable (name, country) VALUES (?, ?)';
$values = array('John Doe', 'US');
$db->execute($sql, $values);
```

See also

▸ Learn more about prepared statements in PHP at `http://php.net/manual/en/mysqli.quickstart.prepared-statements.php`

Creating a custom model class

Writing SQL commands is a quick and easy way to interact with the database in concrete5, but it isn't the best way. Since concrete5 is an **MVC** (**Model View Controller**) application, all data actions should really live in models. A **model** is a representation of an object that exists in the database, which will contain methods to read and write data to that object and have it persist in the database.

In this recipe, we will create a new table called Books, which will contain several book records. We will then create a Book model that will represent book data within the database.

Getting ready

concrete5 follows specific conventions in the naming of database tables. If you open the concrete5 database in an SQL query browser (such as phpMyAdmin or Sequel Pro on OS X), you will see that each of the tables begins with a capital letter and subsequent words in the table name are also camel-cased. In addition, tables should be plural in concrete5, since they contain multiple instances of items. Models should be singular, since they represent an individual item in the database (most of the time). Therefore, the new table that we will create will be called Books and the model will be called Book.

How to do it...

Have a look at the following steps:

1. First, create the `Books` table that we will be using for the new `Book` model. We recommend using a database browser tool such as phpMyAdmin, MySQL Workbench, Sequel Pro (OS X), or Heidi SQL (Windows). The query can also be performed from the following:

```
CREATE TABLE `Books` (
  `id` int(11) unsigned NOT NULL AUTO_INCREMENT,
  `title` varchar(255) NOT NULL DEFAULT '',
  `author` varchar(255) NOT NULL DEFAULT '',
  PRIMARY KEY (`id`)
);
```

2. Create a new file for the `Book` model. In `/models` folder, create a file called `book.php`.

3. Add the `defined` or `die` statement to the top of the file. This is required on all PHP files in concrete5 to prevent scripts from getting executed on their own:

```php
<?php
defined('C5_EXECUTE') or die("Access Denied.");
```

4. Create the class definition for the `Book` model, extending the core `Model` class.

```php
class Book extends Model {

}
```

5. Add a method to create a new book, accepting a title, and author name as parameters:

```php
public function createBook($title, $author) {
  $db = Loader::db();
      $this->title = $title;
  $this->author = $author;
      $query = 'INSERT INTO Books (title, author) VALUES (?, ?)';
  $values = array($title, $author);
      $db->execute($query, $values);
  $this->id = mysql_insert_id();
      return $this->id;
}
```

6. Add another method to load a book by its ID:

```php
public function loadById($id) {
  $db = Loader::db();
  $query = 'SELECT * FROM Books WHERE id = ?';
```

```
    $books = $db->getAll($query, $id);
  // get the first result (there should be only one)
$book = $books[0];
    // set each property of the result to the current object
$this->id = $book['id'];
$this->title = $book['title'];
$this->author = $book['author'];
}
```

7. Finally, add a method to get a book's title:

```
public function getTitle() {
    return $this->title;
}
```

8. Save `book.php`. Now that the `Book` model has been created and saved, let's try using it to write to and read from the database. To keep things simple, we will just stick this code in `/config/site_post.php`.

9. Load the `Book` model using the `Loader` class:

```
Loader::model('book');
```

10. Create a new instance of `Book`:

```
$book = new Book();
```

11. Add a new book to the database using the `createBook` function we declared previously:

```
$book->createBook('concrete5 Cookbook', 'David Strack');
```

12. Get the book's title using the function that we declared.

```
$title = $book->getTitle();
```

How it works...

Let's walk through the code that we just wrote. First, we made sure to create a table in the database called `Books`. This table has three columns, an `ID` field (which auto-increments every time a row is created), a `title` field, and an `author` field.

Next, we created a class called `Book` in `/models/book.php`. This class will represent an instance of an individual record in the `Books` table. The class extends the core `Model` class (which is just a basic implementation defined in `/concrete/core/libraries/model.php`). We then added a method to add new books to the database. The `createBook` method first loaded the database object, then it assigned the `title` and `author` to the current `Book` object. After performing the `INSERT` query, the method sets the book's ID using the `mysql_insert_id()` function. Finally, the function returns the new `ID` of the row we just added.

The `loadById` function was added next. This function will accept an `ID` as the parameter, and then perform a `SELECT` query on the database to find the corresponding row. Notice that in this demonstration we never actually verified that the record exists. In real-world use, you will want to make sure to account for that. Once we have the `Book` object loaded, we assign the three properties (`ID`, `title`, and `author`) to the class object.

Finally, we added a simple getter function to return the title of the book. Note that this function will only work after the `Book` class has been loaded, either by calling `loadById`, or by creating a new book with the `createBook` function.

There's more...

It should be pretty clear that by creating models to handle data object, developers can save a ton of work and keep their code clean. Rather than having SQL statements spread all over the code, all of the database-related logic is contained in the model. This allows for fast and easy creation and access of database rows.

See also

- ▸ The *Loading the database object* recipe
- ▸ The *Retrieving data from the database* recipe
- ▸ The *Writing data to the database* recipe
- ▸ The *Guarding against SQL injections with prepared statements* recipe

Reading from the database with active record

Now that we have created a `Model` class, it is easy to see how this can be a huge benefit to developers, wanting to keep their codebase clean and maintainable. However, we can take this one step further using active record. The reality is, the tasks in the previous recipe could have been performed with less than half of the code that was written.

If you are familiar with frameworks such as Ruby on Rails or CakePHP, then you may have some experience with active record already. **Active record** is a convention of using classes that contain create, update, read, and delete functionality, as well as properties mapped to a record in the database.

In this recipe, we will explore how to use active record to load models from the database.

Getting ready

We will be using the same `Books` table in the database from the previous recipe. If you need to create this table, run the following SQL on your database:

```
CREATE TABLE `Books` (
    `id` int(11) unsigned NOT NULL AUTO_INCREMENT,
    `title` varchar(255) NOT NULL DEFAULT '',
    `author` varchar(255) NOT NULL DEFAULT '',
    PRIMARY KEY (`id`)
);
```

Also, make sure that a record with the ID of `1` exists in that table. If you ran through the previous recipe, it should exist already.

How to do it...

Have a look at the following steps:

1. If the record with the ID of `1` doesn't exist, create a `Book` class in `/models/book.php`.

2. Make sure the contents of `book.php` look like the following:

    ```php
    <?php
    defined('C5_EXECUTE') or die("Access Denied.");
    class Book extends Model {
        public $_table = 'Books';
        public function getTitle() {
            return $this->title;
        }
    }
    ```

3. Now, let's write a little code to make this model come to life. For this demo, we will just be writing the code in `/config/site_post.php` since it is just temporary dummy code.

4. Load the model:

    ```php
    Loader::model('book');
    ```

5. Create a new instance of the `Book` class:

    ```php
    $book = new Book();
    ```

6. Load the book with the ID of `1`:

    ```php
    $book->load('id = ?', '1');
    ```

7. Get the book's title:

    ```php
    $title = $book->getTitle();
    ```

8. Output the title to the screen:

```
echo $title;
exit;
```

How it works...

As you can see, the `Book` model contained no SQL, yet it was still able to perform a lookup on the database and load the book with the ID of `1`. The `Book` class extends the `Model` class, which extends the `ADOdb_Active_Record` class. The `ADOdb_Active_Record` class implements several functions to provide typical read, update, create, and delete functionality.

One important change to note is that early in the class body, we added a member variable called `$_table`. If we would have left that out, everything still would have worked. The `ADOdb_Active_Record` class actually does some basic inflection (converting the singular class name (`Book`) into the plural database table name (`Books`)). However, the inflection is essentially only good at adding `s` to the end of class names and that's about it. More complex pluralizations can fail, so it's a good idea to always specify the table name.

The `load` function of the `ADOdb_Active_Record` class expects the same syntax that one would find in an SQL `WHERE` statement. Writing `load('id = ?')` is equivalent to writing the following prepared statement:

```
SELECT * FROM Books WHERE id = ?
```

The `load` function then assigns all of the properties to the object. It's clear how this can eliminate a lot of code when performing simple **CRUD** tasks in concrete5.

See also

▸ The *Creating a custom model class* recipe
▸ The *Guarding against SQL injections with prepared statements* recipe

Writing to the database with active record

Active record can also be used to write to the database. In this recipe, we will use the `Book` class created in the previous recipe to add a new book record to the database.

Getting ready

Make sure that the `Book` model and `Books` table have been created. Refer to the *Reading from the database with active record* recipe to see how that class should be created.

How to do it...

Have a look at the following steps:

1. We will enter the code in `/config/site_post.php`, so open that file in your code editor.

2. Load the model:

   ```
   Loader::model('book');
   ```

3. Create a new instance of the `Book` class:

   ```
   $book = new Book();
   ```

4. Set the title of the book:

   ```
   $book->title = 'The Wind in the Willows';
   ```

5. Set the author of the book:

   ```
   $book->author = 'Kenneth Grahame';
   ```

6. Save the new book data:

   ```
   $book->save();
   exit;
   ```

How it works...

After setting the `title` and `author` properties to the `Book` object, calling the `save` function will automatically save the item to the database, and creating a new row.

See also

▶ The *Creating a custom model class* recipe
▶ The *Reading from the database with active record* recipe

Updating a database record with active record

Updating database items is very similar to creating them. In this recipe, we will load a book with the ID of 1 and change its title.

Getting ready

This recipe uses the same `Book` model and `Books` table from the previous, the *Reading from the database with active record* recipe. Make sure those files are in place before beginning this recipe.

How to do it...

Have a look at the following steps:

1. Open `/config/site_post.php` in your code editor.

2. Load the model:

   ```
   Loader::model('book');
   ```

3. Create a new instance of the book class:

   ```
   $book = new Book();
   ```

4. Load the book by its ID:

   ```
   $book->load('id = ?', '1');
   ```

5. Change the title of the book:

   ```
   $book->title = 'New Title';
   ```

6. Save the changes to the database:

   ```
   $book->update();
   exit;
   ```

How it works...

Once the book record is loaded, the `ID` property of the object is set. The `Model` class uses this `ID` to update the correct record when `update` is called. If the `ID` of the object doesn't exist or isn't set when `update` is called, a new record will be created.

See also

▶ The *Creating a custom model class* recipe

▶ The *Reading from the database with active record* recipe

Searching the database using active record

Often, web applications will need to retrieve multiple records. In this recipe, we will continue working with the concepts of `Books` stored in the database and retrieve an array of all of the books in the database.

Getting ready

Like the other recipes before this one, we are using the same `Book` model and `Books` table from the previous, the *Reading from the database with active record* recipe. Make sure those files are in place before beginning this recipe.

How to do it...

Have a look at the following steps:

1. Open `/config/site_post.php` in your code editor.
2. Load the model:

   ```
   Loader::model('book');
   ```

3. Create a new instance of the `Book` model:

   ```
   $book = new Book();
   ```

4. Find all of the book records:

   ```
   $books = $book->find('1=1');
   ```

5. Loop through the array and echo each book's title:

   ```
   foreach ($books as $b) {
       echo $b->getTitle().'<br />';
   }
   exit;
   ```

How it works...

The `find` function of the `Model` class searches the database and returns the resulting objects in an array. Since the `find` function is already including `WHERE` in the query, we need to filter by a truth condition to find all of the records, so `1=1` does the job here.

There's more...

The `find` function also supports using prepared statements to search the table. Here, we will look for books that have `'concrete5'` in the title: Have a look at the following:

```
$books = $book->find('title LIKE "%?%"', 'concrete5');
```

See also

- ▶ The *Creating a custom model class* recipe
- ▶ The *Reading from the database with active record* recipe

Deleting objects using active record and model classes

The final facet of CRUD actions with active record is deleting entries. In this recipe, we will load a book with the ID of `1` and delete it from the database.

Getting ready

We will be using the same `Book` model and `Books` table from the previous the *Reading from the database with active record* recipe. Make sure that file is in place before beginning this recipe.

How to do it...

Have a look at the following steps:

1. Open `/config/site_post.php` in your code editor.
2. Load the model:
   ```
   Loader::model('book');
   ```
3. Create a new instance of the model:
   ```
   $book = new Book();
   ```
4. Load the book with the ID of `1`.
   ```
   $book->load('id = ?', '1');
   ```
5. Delete that book:
   ```
   $book->delete();
   exit;
   ```

How it works...

Calling the `delete` function of the `Model` class will run the `DELETE` query on the database, permanently deleting the record associated with that item. Using your preferred SQL browsing tool, you can see that the record has been removed from the database.

See also

▸ The *Creating a custom model class* recipe

▸ The *Reading from the database with active record* recipe

Defining relationships with active record

The primary feature of relational database systems (such as MySQL) is the ability to link data to other bits of data using relationships. Consider a database that stores states and cities in the United States. Each state can have many cities, but each city belongs to only one state. These relationships, "has many" and "belongs to", are definable using concrete5's active record support.

In this recipe, we will link two tables, `States` and `Cities`, and use the relationships to retrieve the related data.

Getting ready

First, we will need to create tables for both `Cities` and `States`. Use the following SQL to populate those tables (this SQL is also available for download from the book's website):

```
CREATE TABLE `Cities` (
  `id` int(11) unsigned NOT NULL AUTO_INCREMENT,
  `name` varchar(255) NOT NULL DEFAULT '',
  `state_id` int(11) NOT NULL,
  PRIMARY KEY (`id`)
);
INSERT INTO `Cities` (`id`, `name`, `state_id`)
VALUES
  (1,'New York',2),
  (2,'Buffalo',2),
  (3,'Green Bay',1),
  (4,'Chicago',3),
  (5,'San Francisco',4),
  (6,'San Diego',4),
  (7,'Oakland',4);
CREATE TABLE `States` (
```

```
  `id` int(11) unsigned NOT NULL AUTO_INCREMENT,
  `name` varchar(255) NOT NULL DEFAULT '',
  PRIMARY KEY (`id`)
);
INSERT INTO `States` (`id`, `name`)
VALUES
  (1,'Wisconsin'),
  (2,'New York'),
  (3,'Illinois'),
  (4,'California');
```

How to do it...

Have a look at the following steps:

1. Create a model for state in `/models/state.php`:

    ```
    class State extends Model {}
    ```

2. Create a model for `city` in `/models/city.php`:

    ```
    class City extends Model {}
    ```

3. At the bottom of the `state` model file (outside of the class body), define the relationship to `city`:

    ```
    Model::ClassHasMany('State', 'Cities','state_id');
    ```

4. Save both of these class files.

5. Now, we will get the cities that belong to California (state with ID = 4).

6. Open `/config/site_post.php` in your code editor, so that we can run some code.

7. Load the `state` model:

    ```
    Loader::model('state');
    ```

8. Create a new instance of the `state` model:

    ```
    $state = new State();
    ```

9. Load the `state` with the ID of 4 (California in our data example):

    ```
    $state->load('id = ?', '4');
    ```

10. Get the state's cities using the active record relationship:

    ```
    $cities = $state->Cities;
    ```

11. Loop through the cities and output each city's name:

```
foreach ($cities as $city) {
    echo $city->name .'<br />';
}
exit;
```

How it works...

The static function called `ClassHasMany` on the `Model` class accepts three parameters. The first parameter is the name of the class that we are assigning this relationship to (in this case, `State`). The second parameter is the name of the database table that contains the child content. The third column is the name of the foreign key, which will be used to determine which rows are children of the parent class.

There's more...

One can also declare `belongs to` relationships in a similar manner.

```
Model::ClassBelongsTo('City','State','state_id','id');
```

See also

- ▶ The *Creating a custom model class* recipe
- ▶ The *Reading from the database with active record* recipe

6
Creating CRUD Interfaces

In this chapter we will cover the following:

- ▶ Creating controller files for single pages on the dashboard
- ▶ Creating view files for single pages on the dashboard
- ▶ Adding single pages to the dashboard
- ▶ Creating a form to create items
- ▶ Saving data to the database from a controller
- ▶ Creating a view to display a list of database items
- ▶ Adding editing capabilities to create a form
- ▶ Creating a delete action

Introduction

One of the features that has made concrete5 such an increasingly popular choice as a content management system is the fact that it allows developers to customize it quickly and easily. A common task when customizing content management systems is to create customized interfaces to allow site editors edit special content in a consistent manner.

Consider a website that manages a list of books in the database. Sure, a site editor could simply maintain this list as a typical block of content, but this can be tedious, and the results aren't guaranteed to be consistent. This is where creating CRUD interfaces can be beneficial.

CRUD (short for create, read, update, and delete) interfaces can easily be added to concrete5 to allow users to easily manage custom data in the database. In this chapter, we will learn how to create CRUD interfaces in the concrete5 dashboard. Combining the different recipes in this chapter will result in a fully functional CRUD to manage blog posts.

CRUD interfaces largely revolve around **single pages**. Single pages in concrete5 are just like regular pages, except that they can have a PHP controller file and a separate view file, allowing for advanced functionality. This allows developers to use MVC conventions and keep their code organized. Single pages are also considered to be more permanent than regular pages, as they aren't added or removed as frequently.

A note about the data in this chapter

The chapter will revolve around managing simple blog posts in the database. To work with this data, execute the following SQL code on your database. The code will also be available for download on the book's website.

```
CREATE TABLE BlogPosts (
   id int(11) unsigned NOT NULL AUTO_INCREMENT,
   title varchar(255) NOT NULL DEFAULT '',
   content longtext NOT NULL,
   post_date datetime NOT NULL,
   PRIMARY KEY (id)
);
INSERT INTO BlogPosts (id, title, content, post_date)
VALUES
   (1,'Hello World','This is my first post!','2013-05-01 13:05:00'),
   (2,'Another Sample Post','Some more great content.','2013-05-10
   14:42:00');
```

Creating controller files for single pages on the dashboard

The first step in creating single pages for use on the dashboard is to create the controller files for each page. Since we will be creating pages to add, edit, and list the blog posts, we will need to add two single pages to the dashboard, a default view (which will list the blog posts) and an add view (which will be a form to add and edit posts).

Getting ready

The names of files and directories are important; concrete5 will need them to match up with the path that displays in the URL of the site. For example, if we want our list of blog posts to appear at `http://example.com/dashboard/posts`, we will have to be conscious of that fact when naming files and classes. In this recipe, we will add single pages to `/dashboard/posts` and `/dashboard/posts/add`.

How to do it...

The steps for creating controller files for simple pages on the dashboard are as follows:

1. Using your operating system's file manager (or your favorite FTP tool or text editor), create a directory in `/controllers` called `dashboard/`.

2. Now, add a file called `posts.php`.

3. Next, add a new directory called `posts/` in `/controllers/dashboard`.

4. Add the controller file for the add/edit form in `/controllers/dashboard/posts/add.php`.

5. Your files and directories should look like the following screenshot:

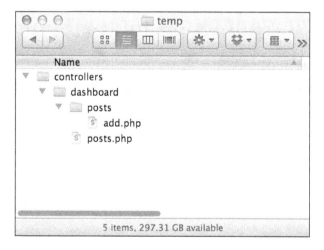

6. Open the `/controllers/dashboard/posts.php` file in your preferred code editor.

7. Declare the controller class, extending the core controller class, as shown in the following code snippet. Save this file and close it.

```
class DashboardPostsController extends Controller {
}
```

8. Open the file in `/controllers/dashboard/posts/add.php`.

9. Declare the class for the form controller, being sure to extend the core controller as well, as shown in the following code snippet. Close this file and save it.

```
class DashboardPostsAddController extends Controller {
}
```

How it works...

concrete5 makes use of the convention over configuration concept when it comes to single pages. Developers simply have to remember how concrete5 expects files to appear and then concrete5 will do all of the work in terms of loading classes and instantiating them. As a result, file and directory names, as well as the class names of the controllers are important. The files we have created here will (eventually) be available at `http://example.com/dashboard/posts` and `http://example.com/dashboard/posts/add`.

See also

▶ The *Creating view files for single pages on the dashboard* recipe
▶ The *Adding single pages to the dashboard* recipe

Creating view files for single pages on the dashboard

Single pages need both controller and view files. Adhering to MVC design principles dictates that the presentation code (HTML) should be separate from the controller logic. Adding view files is very similar to adding controllers, which we learned in the previous recipe.

Getting ready

Just how it was when we added controllers, the file and directory names are important here as well.

How to do it...

The steps for creating view files for simple pages are as follows:

1. Create a new directory in `/single_pages` called `dashboard/`.
2. Add a file called `posts.php` in `/single_pages/dashboard/posts.php`.
3. Add a directory called `posts/` in `/single_pages/dashboard`.
4. Now, create a file called `add.php` in `/single_pages/dashboard/posts/`.

5. The contents of your `single_pages/` directory should look like the following screenshot:

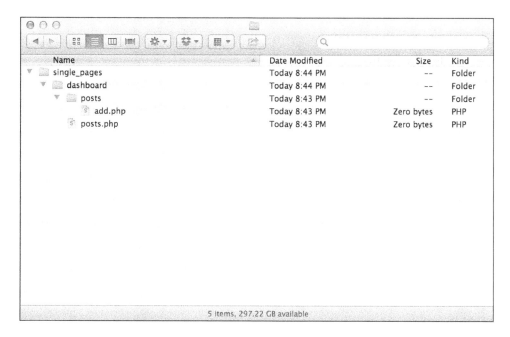

How it works...

The file and directory names should conform to how the pages will appear in the sitemap and in the URLs. The files and directories in this recipe would produce single pages at `http://example.com/dashboard/posts` and `http://example.com/dashboard/posts/add`. The make it PHP files that we added do not need to contain anything yet.

See also

▸ The *Creating controller files for single pages on the dashboard* recipe

▸ The *Adding single pages to the dashboard* recipe

Adding single pages to the dashboard

Once the controller and view files have been created in the concrete5 filesystem, there is still one more step that needs to be performed before we can visit these pages in the browser and begin adding custom CRUD logic. The pages must be added in the concrete5 sitemap so that the CMS knows the pages exist and can direct requests to them.

Getting ready

Before you can add single pages to the site, the view and controller files must exist in the filesystem. Refer to the previous two recipes on how to do this correctly.

How to do it...

1. Go to the single pages manager of the dashboard by visiting `/dashboard/pages/single` (you may be asked to log in). The page will look like the following screenshot:

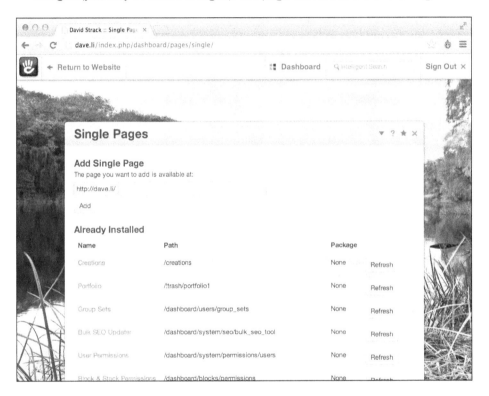

2. Type the path of the posts page (`/dashboard/posts`) and click on **Add**.
3. Type the path of the add page (`/dashboard/posts/add`) and click on **Add**.
4. The pages have now been added and can be viewed by visiting their respective URLs.

How it works...

concrete5 will verify whether the controller and view files exist, and then will add the new single page to the sitemap. This makes the page available to access via URL, and if the page is stored on the dashboard, concrete5 will automatically perform access control checks on the user.

See also

▸ The *Creating controller files for single pages on the dashboard* recipe

▸ The *Creating view files for single pages on the dashboard* recipe

Creating a form to create items

Now that we know how to add bare bones single pages to the dashboard, we can create the real CRUD interfaces. The first interface that we will program is the form for creating and editing blog posts.

Getting ready

First, you will need to make sure that you know how to add controller and view files for the single pages. Refer to the first three recipes in this chapter for guidance on how to do that.

Our blog posts in this chapter will have three fields: `title`, `content`, and `post date`. The `title` and `content` fields will be set by the user with the form in this recipe, and the `post date` will be set by our controller once the form has been submitted.

To keep this chapter on point, much of the irrelevant HTML surrounding our form has been omitted. Refer to the book's website to see the complete HTML code if you are having trouble with the markup of your form.

How to do it...

The steps for creating a form to create items are as follows:

1. Open `/single_pages/dashboard/posts/add.php` in your preferred code editor.

2. We will make use of the form helper, so load that helper at the top of the file.

   ```php
   <?php $form = Loader::helper('form') ?>
   ```

3. Wrap everything in a `div` tag with the class of `ccm-ui` so our form will take advantage of the Bootstrap styles included in concrete5.

   ```
   <div class="ccm-ui">
   ```

4. Use the Dashboard helper to output the appropriate HTML for the header of the form.

```php
<?php
    $dashboard = Loader::helper('concrete/dashboard');
    echo $dashboard->getDashboardPaneHeader('Title');
?>
```

5. Set the form's `action` to the `save` function of the controller and make sure it is sending the data as a `POST` request.

```html
<form action="<?php echo $this->action('save') ?>" method="POST">
```

6. Echo the input for the `title` field.

```php
<?php echo $form->text('title') ?>
```

7. Echo the input for the `content` field.

```php
<?php echo $form->textarea('content') ?>
```

8. Create the submit button.

```html
<input class="btn btn-primary" type="submit" value="Save">
```

9. Create a cancel button and have it take the user back to the posts listing when clicked.

```html
<a href="<?php echo $this->url('/dashboard/posts') ?>"
class="btn">Cancel</a>
```

10. Save the `add.php` view file, as it is time to move to the controller.

How it works...

The `add.php` view file is an interface for a concrete5 `View` object. As a result, the `$this` keyword is set to an instance of the `View` class. Using functions such as `action` and `url` on the `$this` keyword will generate URLs that are aware of the concrete5 site's settings, such as if the site has pretty URLs enabled, or if the site is located in a sub-directory.

Using the Form helper, we can quickly output the fields that we need to display on the form. The Form helper will be even more useful when we add the ability to edit data, which will happen later in this chapter.

There's more...

As mentioned at the beginning of this chapter, most of the boilerplate HTML surrounding the form here was left out of the chapter. Please download the complete source code from the book's website if you wish to see how the entire page is structured.

See also

▸ The *Creating controller files for single pages on the dashboard* recipe

▸ The *Creating view files for single pages on the dashboard* recipe

▸ The *Adding single pages to the dashboard* recipe

▸ The *Loading a helper class* recipe in *Chapter 4, Using the Core Helpers*

▸ The *Creating custom forms with the Form helper* recipe in *Chapter 4, Using the Core Helpers*

▸ The *Saving data to the database from a controller* recipe

Saving data to the database from a controller

Once you have the HTML (and related helper PHP) for your form created, it is time to make that form do something. In the previous recipe, we set the action of our HTML form to the `save` action of the controller. In this recipe, we will write the code of that save action, so that our blog posts will be stored in the database once the save button is clicked.

Getting ready

This recipe is continuing the chapter's theme of creating a CRUD interface for managing simple blog posts. Make sure the previous recipes in this chapter have been completed before working on this part. Also, make sure that the database table specified in the chapter introduction exists.

How to do it...

The steps for saving data to the database from a controller are as follows:

1. Create a new model in `/models/blog_post.php`.

2. Open `/models/blog_post.php` in your code editor and create the `BlogPost` class.

```
class BlogPost extends Model {
    var $_table = 'BlogPosts';
}
```

3. Open `/controllers/dashboard/posts/add.php` in your preferred code or text editor.

4. Define the `save` function.

```
public function save() {
}
```

5. In the `save` function, load the `BlogPost` model.

   ```
   Loader::model('blog_post');
   ```

6. Create a new instance of the `BlogPost` model.

   ```
   $post = new BlogPost();
   ```

7. Set the `title` to the value that was submitted in the HTTP POST request.

   ```
   $post->title = $this->post('title');
   ```

8. Set the `content` to the value that was submitted in the form POST request.

   ```
   $post->content = $this->post('content');
   ```

9. Set the `post date` to the current date/time.

   ```
   $post->post_date = date('YYYY-MM-DD H:i:s');
   ```

10. Save the model.

    ```
    $post->save();
    ```

11. Redirect the user to the listing of the posts, which will indicate that the save was successful.

    ```
    $this->redirect('/dashboard/posts');
    ```

How it works...

The `save` function is run whenever an HTTP request (GET or POST) is made to `/dashboard/posts/add/save`, and that is exactly where the HTML form sends its data when it is submitted. We load the `BlogPost` model and set each of its attributes, finally saving the new item to the database and redirecting the user to the post listing.

There's more...

In real life usage, you would want to use the Validation Helper to make sure that users have filled out the form correctly and that both the title and content fields were not empty.

See also

▸ The *Creating controller files for single pages on the dashboard* recipe

▸ The *Creating view files for single pages on the dashboard* recipe

▸ The *Adding single pages to the dashboard* recipe

▸ The *Creating a form to create items* recipe

▸ *Chapter 5, Working with Databases and Models*

Creating a view to display a list of database items

Now that we can add items to our database, it sure would be nice to have an interface to show what items already exist in our table, and to add, edit, and delete those items from there.

In this recipe, we will handle the Read aspect of CRUD interfaces by creating an HTML table that lists all of the blog posts stored in the database, as well as provide buttons to edit and delete those items.

Getting ready

As with the rest of the recipes in this chapter, we will be dealing with simple blog posts. Make sure that the previous recipes have been completed prior to working with this recipe, otherwise there may be a step missing!

Some of the boilerplate HTML in this recipe has been omitted from this chapter in order to keep the focus on the code that is important to know. The website for this book does contain a complete source code download that will allow you to explore the entire HTML code in this interface.

How to do it...

The steps for creating a view to display a list of database items are as follows:

1. Open `/controllers/dashboard/posts.php` in your preferred text editor.
2. Define the `view` function, which will automatically get run when the page loads.

   ```
   public function view() {
   }
   ```

3. In the `view` function, load the `BlogPost` model.

   ```
   Loader::model('blog_post');
   ```

4. Create a new instance of `BlogPost`.

   ```
   $post = new BlogPost();
   ```

5. Find all of the blog posts by passing a truthy condition (1=1) to the `find` function.

   ```
   $posts = $post->find('1=1');
   ```

6. Set a variable called `$posts` on the view that is equal to the results of the model query.

   ```
   $this->set('posts', $posts);
   ```

7. Save the controller file.

8. Open the posts index view which is located at `/single_pages/dashboard/posts.php`

9. Make sure to create a `div` tag that has a class of `ccm-ui` in order to make use of the built-in Bootstrap styles.

```
<div class="ccm-ui">
```

10. Use the Dashboard helper to generate the HTML for the header section.

```php
<?php
  $dashboard = Loader::helper('concrete/dashboard');
  echo $dashboard->getDashboardPaneHeader('Blog Posts');
?>
```

11. Create a table to hold the posts.

```
<table class="table table-striped table-bordered">
```

12. We will need headings for the four columns we will be displaying.

```
<th>ID</th>
<th>Title</th>
<th>Post Date</th>
<th>Actions</th>
```

13. Loop through the `$posts` variable that was set in the controller and output each row of posts. The last column will contain the buttons to edit or delete each post.

```php
<?php foreach ($posts as $post): ?>
  <tr>
    <td><?php echo $post->id ?></td>
    <td><?php echo $post->title ?></td>
    <td><?php echo date('DATE_APP_GENERIC_MDY_FULL,
    strtotime($post->post_date)) ?></td>
    <td>
      <a href="<?php echo $this-
      >url('/dashboard/posts/add/edit/', $post->id) ?>"
      class="btn">Edit</a>
      <a href="<?php echo $this-
      >action('/dashboard/posts/delete/', $post->id) ?>"
      class="btn danger">Delete</a>
    </td>
  </tr>
<?php endforeach; ?>
```

14. Save the view file.

How it works...

When an HTTP GET or POST request is made to /dashboard/posts/, the view function on the posts controller is automatically executed. In this function, we load data from the BlogPost model, and then send that data to the view. This allows us to keep the real business logic out of our view files and create more reusable and maintainable code.

See also

- ▸ The *Creating controller files for single pages on the dashboard* recipe
- ▸ The *Creating view files for single pages on the dashboard* recipe
- ▸ The *Adding single pages to the dashboard* recipe
- ▸ The *Creating a form to create items* recipe
- ▸ The *Saving data to the database from a controller* recipe

Adding editing capabilities to create a form

Now that we have added the ability to create and view items, it is time for the third facet of CRUD interfaces: editing. In this recipe, we will implement the logic necessary to be able to edit items using the form that we created in the recipe *Creating a form to create item*.

Getting ready

As with the rest of the recipes in this chapter, this recipe revolves around the concept of managing simple blog posts, each with a title, a block of content text, and a post date. Make sure that the previous recipes have been completed before embarking on this latest journey! The MySQL data for this recipe is also included at the beginning of this chapter as well as on the book's website.

How to do it...

The steps for adding editing capabilities to create a form are as follows:

1. Open the controller file for the add form (located at /controllers/dashboard/posts/add.php).

2. Declare the edit function, with a single parameter for the ID parameter of the post to edit.

```
public function edit($id) {
}
```

3. In the `edit` function, load the `blog post` model.

```
Loader::model('blog_post');
```

4. Create a new instance of the `model` class.

```
$post = new BlogPost();
```

5. Load the `post` object using the `ID` parameter that was passed in via the edit URL.

```
$post->load('id = ?', $id);
```

6. Set the `post` variable to the view, casting the `post` object into an array to prevent the add form from breaking when there is no post object set.

```
$this->set($post, (array) $post);
```

7. In the `save` function of the controller, add the following code just below `$post = new BlogPost();`

```
if ($this->post('id')) {
   $post->load('id = ?', $this->post('id'));
}
```

8. Change the `save` function call to use the `replace` function.

```
$post->replace();
```

9. Save the controller file.

10. Open the `view` file, located at `/single_pages/dashboard/posts/add.php`

11. Add a second parameter to the `title` input that will populate the field with the post's title if it exists.

```
<?php echo $form->text('title', $post['title']) ?>
```

12. Add a second parameter to the `content` input that will pre-fill the contents when the form is in edit mode.

```
<?php echo $form->textarea('content', $post['content']) ?>
```

13. Just below the closing table tag, add the following snippet to add a hidden input when the form is in edit mode:

```
<?php if ($post['id']): ?>
   <?php echo $form->hidden('id', $post['id']) ?>
<?php endif; ?>
```

14. Save the `view` file.

How it works...

When a request is made to the URL `/dashboard/posts/add/edit/<id>`, concrete5 will automatically fire the `edit` function of the controller and pass the `ID` parameter as the first parameter. Then we can load the corresponding model and send the data to the view. We need to cast the post data into an array so that the form will still work even if it is not in edit mode.

We also add a little snippet to the `save` function to make sure that if there is an ID included in the `POST` request, then we need to save an existing post rather than create a new one. By changing the `save` function call to `replace`, we are telling the model to create a brand new record if one does not exist, otherwise it will simply update the existing model.

There's more...

In real life usage, it would be smart to check the `ID` parameter in the edit function to make sure that it is set. Also, it would be a good idea to handle requests in which a post is loaded that doesn't exist.

See also

- The *Creating controller files for single pages on the dashboard* recipe
- The *Creating view files for single pages on the dashboard* recipe
- The *Adding single pages to the dashboard* recipe
- The *Creating a form to create items* recipe
- The *Saving data to the database from a controller* recipe

Creating a delete action

The final pillar of the CRUD Interface is the ability to delete items. In concrete5, this is a little bit more simple than the other CRUD tasks, as deleting items typically doesn't require a visual component. In this recipe, we will delete a blog post and simply redirect the user back to the index view of the posts.

Getting ready

We will continue working with the concept of simple blog posts. This recipe assumes that you have completed the previous recipes in this chapter and have the appropriate database tables created.

How to do it...

1. Open the controller file located at `/controllers/dashboard/posts.php`.

2. Declare a new function called `delete` that has one parameter, `$id`.

```
public function delete($id) {
}
```

3. In the `delete` function, load the `blog posts` model.

```
Loader::model('blog_post');
```

4. Create a new instance of the model.

```
$post = new BlogPost();
```

5. Load the post by its ID.

```
$post->load('id = ?', $id);
```

6. Delete the post by calling the `delete` function.

```
$post->delete();
```

7. Redirect the user back to the posts index.

```
$this->redirect('/dashboard/posts');
```

How it works...

When a request is made to `/dashboard/posts/delete/<id>`, the `delete` function of the posts controller is executed. In this controller, we simply load a post by its ID, and then call the built-in `delete` function of the model. Then, we just redirect users back to the post listing.

There's more...

It would be wise to verify that the post with the specified ID exists before deleting. Also, most users would expect some kind of confirmation dialogue before performing such a destructive action, so that would be a nice thing to add in a real life situation.

See also

▶ The *Creating controllers for single pages on the dashboard* recipe

▶ The *Creating view files for single pages on the dashboard* recipe

▶ The *Adding single pages to the dashboard* recipe

7
Working with Users and Permissions

In this chapter we will cover the following:

- ▶ Checking if the current user is logged in
- ▶ Getting the currently logged-in user
- ▶ Loading a user by its ID
- ▶ Loading a user by its username
- ▶ Getting a user's info
- ▶ Setting a user's attributes
- ▶ Retrieving a user's attributes
- ▶ Loading a group by its ID
- ▶ Loading a group by its name
- ▶ Adding a user to a group
- ▶ Getting all of the users from a group
- ▶ Checking if a user is a member of a group
- ▶ Removing a user from a group
- ▶ Logging out a user
- ▶ Deleting a user
- ▶ Getting the permission object
- ▶ Checking if a user can write to a page
- ▶ Checking if a user can edit a page
- ▶ Checking a user's file permissions

Introduction

One of concrete5's greatest attributes is the included functionality surrounding users and permissions. concrete5 makes it easy to control which users and user groups can access specific pages. Users in concrete5 can be site editors, administrators, community members, or any other role that site owners can devise.

In this chapter, we will explore several recipes that allow developers to interact with and manipulate user objects, groups, and their related permissions. The recipes in this chapter will empower concrete5 developers to incorporate the powerful user and permissions model into their own custom applications and websites.

Checking if the current user is logged in

One of the most common tasks in concrete5 development is finding out if a user is logged into the website. In this recipe, we will output some HTML to say hello to the logged-in user if they are logged in. If they are logged out, we will output a link to the login page.

How to do it...

The steps for checking if the current user is logged in are as follows:

1. Check if the current user is logged in.

```
$isLoggedIn = User::isLoggedIn();
```

2. If they are logged in, show a welcome message.

```
if ($isLoggedIn) {
  echo '<p>Thanks for logging in!</p>';
}
```

3. Otherwise, show a link to the login page.

```
else {
  echo '<a href="/login">Login</a>';
}
```

How it works...

The user model contains a static function called `isLoggedIn` which will simply return a Boolean result. This does not bring any sort of permission checks into the mix, only checks to see if the person viewing the page is logged in at all.

Getting the currently logged-in user

concrete5 makes it easy to get the object of the currently logged-in user. In this recipe, we will output the the username of the currently logged-in user.

Getting ready

It is a good idea to make sure the user is logged in at all before attempting to display their username. We will use the skills from the previous recipe to make sure the user is logged first.

How to do it...

The steps for getting the currently logged-in user are as follows:

1. Check if the user is logged in.

    ```
    $isLoggedIn = User::isLoggedIn();
    ```

2. If the user is logged in, create a new instance of the `User` class.

    ```
    $user = new User();
    ```

3. Echo the username of the `user` object.

    ```
    echo $user->getUsername();
    ```

How it works...

concrete5 makes it incredibly easy to get the currently logged-in user. Essentially, we only have to instantiate the `User` class, which will return an object representing the currently logged-in user.

See also

- ▸ The *Checking if the current user is logged in* recipe
- ▸ The *Getting a user's info* recipe

Loading a user by its ID

Developers can also load users by their unique IDs. In this recipe, we will load the user with the ID of 1 and output their username.

The steps for loading a user by its ID are as follows:

1. Determine the ID of the user that you wish to load. In this example, we will load the user with an ID of 1.

   ```
   $userId = 1;
   ```

2. Load a user by its ID.

   ```
   $user = User::getByUserID($userId);
   ```

3. Echo out the user's username.

   ```
   echo $user->getUserName();
   ```

How it works...

concrete5 will look in the `Users` table of the database and return a user object populated with data from that corresponding record.

See also

   ▶   The *Loading a user by its username* recipe

Loading a user by its username

In addition to being able to load users by their IDs, developers can also load users by their usernames. In this recipe, we will load a user with the username of admin and output their numerical ID.

How to do it...

The steps for loading a user by its username are as follows:

1. Determine the username of the user that you are loading.

   ```
   $username = 'admin';
   ```

2. Load the user by its username.

   ```
   $user = UserInfo::getByUserName($username);
   ```

3. Echo the user's ID.

   ```
   echo $user->getUserID();
   ```

How it works...

Hey, that was easy! The `UserInfo` class contains methods to load a user by its username rather than just its ID. The `UserInfo` class also has a method to get the numerical user ID, for the user.

See also

▸ The *Loading a user by its ID* recipe
▸ The *Getting the currently logged-in user* recipe

Getting a user's info

User objects carry a lot of information with them, including the user's username, e-mail, and several other attributes. In this recipe, we will run through several functions to retrieve data associated with users.

Getting ready

The code for this chapter doesn't necessarily belong to any specific place in concrete5. The steps for this recipe are basic, one-line functions to demonstrate the different ways to get data from a user object. If you'd like a place to just write arbitrary code and have concrete5 evaluate it, the `site_post.php` file in `config/` is a pretty good place to start.

How to do it...

The steps for getting a user's info are as follows:

1. First, we will load the currently logged-in user.

   ```
   $user = new User();
   ```

2. Get the user's ID.

   ```
   $userId = $user->getUserID();
   ```

3. Get the user's username.

   ```
   $username = $user->getUserName();
   ```

4. Check if the user is registered on the site.

   ```
   $isRegistered = $user->isRegistered();
   ```

5. Check if the user's account is active.

   ```
   $isActive = $user->isActive();
   ```

6. Check if the user is the super admin.

   ```
   $isSuper = $user->isSuperUser();
   ```

7. Load the `UserInfo` object, which contains even more information about the user.

   ```
   $userInfo = UserInfo::getByID($userId);
   ```

8. Get the user's e-mail address.

   ```
   $email = $userInfo->getUserEmail();
   ```

9. Get the user's encrypted password.

   ```
   $password = $userInfo->getUserPassword();
   ```

10. Get the number of times the user has logged in.

    ```
    $loginCount = $userInfo->getNumLogins();
    ```

11. Find out if the user has verified their e-mail address.

    ```
    $verifiedEmail = $userInfo->isValidated();
    ```

12. Get the Unix timestamp of the previous time that this user logged in.

    ```
    $previousLogin = $userInfo->getPreviousLogin();
    ```

13. Find out if the user has an avatar uploaded to the site.

    ```
    $hasAvatar = $userInfo->hasAvatar();
    ```

14. Find out when the user was added to the website.

    ```
    $dateAdded = $userInfo->getUserDateAdded();
    ```

How it works...

The `User` class contains a couple of methods to retrieve basic user data, such as a user's ID and username. When developers want to see more information about a user, though, they will need to use the `UserInfo` class.

See also

▸   The *Getting the currently logged-in user* recipe

Setting a user's attributes

Users in concrete5 can have custom attributes that get defined through the interface. Imagine a website where you would like to know your users' ages. concrete5 does not provide an age field for users out of the box, but one can easily be added using attributes.

Getting ready

First, you will want to make sure that the attribute exists in the concrete5 site before trying to set it. Go to `http://example.com/dashboard/users/attributes` (replacing `example.com` with your own domain name, of course) and make sure that the attribute that you are creating exists. The page will look similar to the following screenshot:

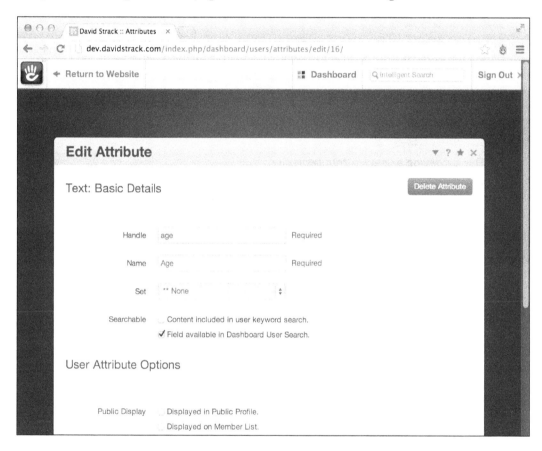

In this recipe, we will work with an attribute with the handle of age, so feel free to create that attribute to follow along.

How to do it...

The steps for setting a user's attributes are as follows:

1. Load the currently logged-in user.

   ```
   $user = new User();
   ```

2. Load the `UserInfo` object for that user.

```
$userInfo = UserInfo::getByUserID($user->getUserID());
```

3. Set the age attribute to `35`.

```
$userInfo->setAttribute('age', 35);
```

How it works...

The `UserInfo` class contains a function called `setAttribute` which will accept either a string that represents the attribute key handle, or an actual instance of an `AttributeKey` object. In this recipe, we opted for the simpler approach of providing the attribute handle in a string.

See also

▸ The *Retrieving a user's attributes* recipe

▸ The *Getting the currently logged-in user* recipe

▸ The *Getting a user's info* recipe

Retrieving a user's attributes

In addition to setting attributes, we can also retrieve them. In this recipe, we will retrieve the attribute for the user's age, which we set in the previous recipe.

Getting ready

As in the previous recipe, you will need to make sure that any attributes you are retrieving actually exist in concrete5. In this case, we will be referencing an attribute with the handle of `age`. If your concrete5 system does not have a user attribute available called age, please adapt this recipe to fit your needs.

How to do it...

The steps for retrieving a user's attributes are as follows:

1. Load the currently logged-in user.

```
$user = new User();
```

2. Get the `user info` object for the user.

```
$userInfo = UserInfo::getByID($user->getUserID());
```

3. Get the value of the user's age attribute.

```
$age = $userInfo->getAttribute('age');
```

How it works...

concrete5 provides a simple API to retrieve attributes from users. In the database, attribute keys and values are spread over several tables and are difficult to query manually. This method is the preferred way to retrieve user attributes.

There's more...

concrete5 also makes use of "magic methods" to retrieve user attributes. Essentially, call a function with the camel-cased version of the attribute handle, preceded by the word get. In this recipe, to get the user's age, we could simply write the following code:

```
$age = $userInfo->getAge();
```

See also

▸ The *Setting a user's attributes* recipe

▸ The *Getting the currently logged-in user* recipe

▸ The *Getting a user's info* recipe

Loading a group by its ID

Groups in concrete5 are ways to organize users by their role on the website. Groups can receive permission settings just like users can. In this recipe, we will load a group with the ID of 3 (which is the Administrators' group on most concrete5 installations).

How to do it...

The steps for loading a group by its ID are as follows:

1. Determine the ID of the group that we want to load.

```
$groupId = 3;
```

2. Load the group by its ID.

```
$group = Group::getByID($groupId);
```

3. Dump the name of the group variable to ensure that it has loaded correctly.

```
echo $group->gName;
exit;
```

How it works...

concrete5 will simply query the `Groups` table in the database to find the group record that corresponds to the provided ID.

See also

▸   The *Loading a group by its name* recipe

Loading a group by its name

Groups can be loaded by their name, which can be useful when you do not know the numeric ID of the group.

How to do it...

The steps for loading a group by its name are as follows:

1.   Define the name of the group that you wish to load.

    ```
    $groupName = 'Administrators';
    ```

2.   Load the group by its name.

    ```
    $group = Group::getByName($groupName);
    ```

3.   Dump the group variable to make sure that you have loaded the group correctly.

    ```
    var_dump($group);
    ```

How it works...

concrete5 queries the database to find the group that has the same name that you provided to the `getByName` function. Group names can be changed through the concrete5 dashboard any time, so use caution when hardcoding group names in your applications.

See also

▸   The *Loading a group by its ID* recipe

Adding a user to a group

While the concrete5 dashboard provides a simple interface to add users to different groups, sometimes you will encounter the need to do it programmatically. In this recipe, we will add a user with the ID of 1 to the Administrators' group, which has an ID of 3.

How to do it...

The steps for adding a user to a group are as follows:

1. Define the ID of the user that you would like to load.
   ```
   $userId = 1;
   ```

2. Load the user by its ID.
   ```
   $user = User::getByID($userId);
   ```

3. Define the ID of the group that you would like to add the user to.
   ```
   $groupId = 3;
   ```

4. Load the group by its ID.
   ```
   $group = Group::getByID($groupId);
   ```

5. Add the user to the group.
   ```
   $user->enterGroup($group);
   ```

How it works...

When the `enterGroup` function of the user model is called, the user will be added to the group that was passed as the first parameter. The user now will inherit all of the permissions associated with that group.

See also

- The *Loading a user by its ID* recipe
- The *Loading a group by its ID* recipe
- The *Removing a user from a group* recipe

Getting all of the users from a group

Once you have loaded a group object, you can easily iterate through the users that are members of that group. In this recipe, we will load a group, and then output the username of each member within the group.

How to do it...

The steps for getting all of the users from a group are as follows:

1. Define the ID of the group that you wish to load.

   ```
   $groupId = 3;
   ```

2. Load the group by its ID.

   ```
   $group = Group::getByID($groupId);
   ```

3. Get an array of group members.

   ```
   $members = $group->getGroupMembers();
   ```

4. Loop through the members array, echoing the user's name.

   ```
   foreach ($members as $member) {
     echo $member->getUserName().'<br />';
   }
   ```

How it works...

As usual, concrete5 does the heavy lifting here in regards to querying the database to find all of the user accounts that are members of the group that has been loaded. The `getGroupMembers` function returns an array of `UserInfo` objects, which can be used to read and modify the members of the group.

See also

▶ The *Loading a group by its ID* recipe
▶ The *Getting a user's info* recipe

Checking if a user is a member of a group

concrete5 comes with a robust permissions model, but sometimes developers will want to do simple permissions and access control tasks on their own. In this recipe, we will see if a user is in the Administrators' group. We will then display a message that indicates if they are an administrator or not.

How to do it...

The steps for checking if a user is a member of a group are as follows:

1. Load the currently logged-in user.

   ```
   $user = new User();
   ```

2. Determine the ID of the group that you wish to load (in this case, it's the Administrators' group with an ID of 3).

   ```
   $groupId = 3; // administrators
   ```

3. Load the group by its ID.

   ```
   $group = Group::getByID($groupId);
   ```

4. Check if the user is a member of the group.

   ```
   $isAdmin = $user->inGroup($group);
   ```

5. Display a message to the user confirming or denying if they are a member of the Administrators' group.

   ```
   if ($isAdmin) {
     echo 'You\'re an administrator!';
   }
   else {
     echo 'You are not an administrator.';
   }
   ```

How it works...

concrete5 checks to see if the user is a member of the specified group object and returns a Boolean value.

See also

  ▶ The *Loading a group by its ID* recipe
  ▶ The *Getting the currently logged-in user* recipe

Removing a user from a group

In addition to being able to add users to groups, concrete5 also allows developers to perform the opposite task: removing users from groups. In this recipe, we will remove a user from the Administrators' group.

How to do it...

The steps for removing a user from a group are as follows:

1. Load the currently logged-in user.

   ```
   $user = new User();
   ```

2. Define the ID of the group that you wish to load.

   ```
   $groupId = 3; // administrators
   ```

3. Load the group by its ID.

   ```
   $group = Group::getByID($groupId);
   ```

4. Check to see if this user is a member of the group.

   ```
   $inGroup = $user->inGroup($group);
   ```

5. If the user is a member, remove them from the group.

   ```
   if ($inGroup) {
     $user->exitGroup($group);
   }
   ```

How it works...

In this case concrete5 will simply remove the association between the user and the group. The user will lose all of the permissions that it had inherited from the group.

See also...

- ▸ The *Adding a user to a group* recipe
- ▸ The *Loading a group by its ID* recipe
- ▸ The *Getting the currently logged-in user* recipe
- ▸ The *Checking if a user is a member of a group* recipe

Logging out a user

concrete5 also contains functionality to log users out of the system programmatically. In this recipe, we will log out the user who is currently logged in.

How to do it...

The steps for logging out a user are as follows:

1. Check if the user is logged in.

```
$loggedIn = User::isLoggedIn();
```

2. Load the logged-in user.

```
$user = new User();
```

3. Log out the user.

```
if ($loggedIn) {
    $user->logout();
}
```

How it works...

concrete5 deletes the current session, effectively logging the user out.

See also

▸ The *Checking if the current user is logged in* recipe
▸ The *Getting the currently logged-in user* recipe

Deleting a user

In this recipe, we will load a user with the ID of 3 and delete that user from concrete5.

How to do it...

The steps for deleting a user are as follows:

1. Define the ID of the user that you wish to delete.

```
$userId = 3;
```

2. Load the UserInfo object for that user.

```
$user = UserInfo::getByID($userId);
```

3. Delete the user.

```
$user->delete();
```

How it works...

concrete5 will remove the user as well as all of their attributes from the database. This action is permanent and cannot be reversed, short of restoring a database backup.

See also

▶ The *Getting a user's info* recipe

Getting the permission object

Verifying and modifying page permissions, centers around the permissions object. In this recipe, we will load the permissions object for a page.

How to do it...

The steps for getting the permission object are as follows:

1. Specify the path of the page for which you want to check the permissions settings.

   ```
   $path = '/about';
   ```

2. Load the page by its path.

   ```
   $page = Page::getByPath($path);
   ```

3. Load the permissions object for that page.

   ```
   $permissions = new Permissions($page);
   ```

4. Dump the permissions object to verify its contents.

   ```
   var_dump($permissions);
   ```

How it works...

concrete5 will return a permissions object that can be further used to determine if a user has access to perform various actions on that page.

There's more...

You can get the permissions objects for content areas and blocks as well, just pass a block or area object to the Permissions constructor instead of a Page object.

See also

 ▸   The *Getting a Page object by its path* in *Chapter 1*, *Pages and Page Types*

Checking if a user can read a page

You may find that sometimes you will want to manually find out if a user is allowed to read a particular page. In this recipe, we will load a page by its path, get the `permissions` object for it, and then find out if the user is allowed to view it.

How to do it...

The steps for checking if a user can read a page are as follows:

1.   Determine the path of the page to load.

```
$path = '/about';
```

2.   Load the page by its path.

```
$page = Page::getByPath($path);
```

3.   Load the `permissions` object for that page.

```
$permissions = new Permissions($page);
```

4.   Find out if the user is allowed to read that page.

```
$canRead = $permissions->canRead();
var_dump($canRead);
exit;
```

How it works...

concrete5 will check all of the permissions for that `Page` object, including group and user permissions, to find out if the current user is allowed to view that page. The *canRead* function returns a Boolean value.

There's more...

Read permissions can also be checked for content areas and blocks by simply providing an area or block object to the `Permissions` constructor, instead of a `Page` object.

See also

▸ The *Getting a Page object by its path* in *Chapter 1, Pages and Page Types*
▸ The *Getting the permission object* recipe

Checking if a user can edit a page

In addition to being able to check if users can view pages, developers can also manually check to see if the logged-in user has the ability to edit a page. In this recipe, we will load a page by its path, get the `permissions` object for that page, and then find out if the user is allowed to edit it.

How to do it...

The steps for checking if a user can edit a page are as follows:

1. Specify the page path to load.
   ```
   $path = '/about';
   ```

2. Load the page.
   ```
   $page = Page::getByPath($path);
   ```

3. Load the `permissions` object for the page.
   ```
   $permissions = new Permissions($page);
   ```

4. Find out if the user can edit the page.
   ```
   $canEdit = $permissions->canWrite();
   var_dump($canEdit);
   exit;
   ```

How it works...

concrete5 will look at the user's own permission settings as well as the settings for any groups that it is a member of, and determine if the user has the ability to edit or write to the given page.

There's more...

As with read permissions, content area and block permissions can also be checked using this method. Simply provide an instance of an area or block instead of a page, and the permissions will be checked against those items instead.

See also

▸ The *Getting a Page object by its path* recipe

▸ The *Getting the permission object* recipe

Checking a user's file permissions

concrete5 allows site owners to specify permissions on the file manager. In this recipe, we will see if a user is allowed to upload files to the file manager.

How to do it...

The steps for checking a user's file permissions are as follows:

1. Load the `FilePermissions` global object.

   ```
   $permissions = FilePermissions::getGlobal();
   ```

2. Check if the user can view the `file manager` interface.

   ```
   $canUpload = $permissions->canAddFiles();
   ```

3. Check if the user can upload to the file manager.

   ```
   $canViewFileManager = $permissions->canAccessFileManager();
   ```

How it works...

The `FilePermissions` class extends the `Permissions` class, and allows users to check the global settings of the file manager.

There's more...

concrete5 also allows developers to check if a user is allowed to upload files of a specific type.

```
$canUploadMp3 = $permissions->canAddFileType('mp3');
```

8

Working with Themes and Add-ons

In this chapter we will cover the following:

- ▶ Creating a custom theme
- ▶ Including the concrete5 required scripts and styles
- ▶ Defining editable content areas
- ▶ Creating page type templates
- ▶ Using elements for repeated portions of HTML
- ▶ Customizing system pages
- ▶ Creating a custom add-on package
- ▶ Using the package controller to execute custom code

Introduction

concrete5 is a little different from other content management systems. Of course, it has world-class inline editing capabilities and a powerful development framework, but it also is incredibly easy to create custom themes and add-ons. Developers and designers can even sell their creations in the concrete5 marketplace. In this chapter, we will learn how to create a very basic theme and also how to create a simple add-on package. Though each of these recipes has its own purpose, it might be useful for beginners to run through the recipes in order to make sure all of the required knowledge is attained.

Creating a custom theme

Themes are an essential part of any content management system, and for good reason. Nobody wants their site to look just like all of the other websites out there. concrete5 comes with a handful of decent-looking themes, but many times you or your clients will want a custom theme developed. The subject of creating themes can actually become quite lengthy and there have been entire books dedicated to this (the book *Creating concrete5 Themes*, by Remo Laubacher, Packt Publishing is highly recommended). In this recipe, we will only demonstrate the minimum requirements to create a custom theme in concrete5.

Getting ready

The complete basic theme code for this recipe is available for free on the website for this book.

How to do it...

The steps for creating a custom theme are as follows:

1. Create a new directory in `/themes` called `basic_theme`.

2. Create a file in `basic_theme` called `description.txt`.

3. Place the title of the theme on the first line of the description file.

   `Basic Theme`

4. Place a short description of the theme on the second line of the text file.

   `This theme is extremely basic`

5. Save the `description.txt` file.

6. Create a new file in `/themes/basic_theme` called `default.php`.

7. Enter the following basic HTML code in the file:

```
<!DOCTYPE html>
<html>
  <head>
    <title>My Super Basic Theme</title>
  </head>
  <body>
    <h1>Hi, this is my super basic theme. It's really
    boring.</h1>
  </body>
</html>
```

8. Save `default.php`.

9. Create a file called `view.php` and keep it empty.

10. Visit the themes area of your site's dashboard at `http://example.com/dashboard/pages/themes`.

11. Click on the **Install** button of your new theme. The page will look like the following screenshot:

12. Click on **Activate** and then on **OK** to apply the theme to all of the pages in your site.

13. You website should now look like the following screenshot:

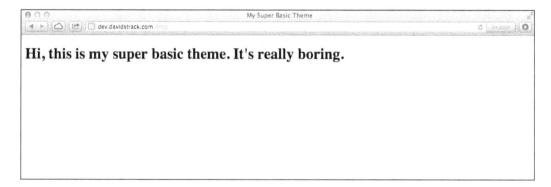

How it works...

concrete5 only requires that the files `description.txt`, `default.php`, and `view.php` need to exist in a theme. The file `description.txt` contains the themes title and description.

There's more...

Obviously this would be unusable for real-life use. There's nowhere to put content! Where's the concrete5 edit bar? The next few recipes will expand on this simple theme to make it a real concrete5 theme.

See also

▶ The *Including the concrete5 required scripts and styles* recipe

▶ The *Using elements for repeated portions of HTML* recipe

▶ The *Defining editable content areas* recipe

Including the concrete5 required scripts and styles

You may have noticed that after creating the extremely simple theme in the previous recipe, the concrete5 edit bar that normally appears at the top of the screen, has gone away. This is because the theme did not include the required collection of JavaScript and CSS files, that concrete5 needs to do its job. In this recipe, we will add the necessary code to include those components in our simple theme.

Getting ready

This recipe will build upon the code of the simple theme from the previous recipe. Feel free to download the source code from the book's website to catch up, or adapt this recipe to fit your own theme.

How to do it...

The steps for including the concrete5 required scripts and styles are as follows:

1. Open the `/themes/basic_theme/default.php` file where our theme's HTML was stored.

2. Remove the `<title>` tag, as we will not need it any longer.

3. Just before the closing `</head>` tag, add the following code to the file:

   ```php
   <?php Loader::element('header_required') ?>
   ```

4. Just before the closing `</body>` tag, add the following code to the file:

   ```php
   <?php Loader::element('footer_required') ?>
   ```

5. Refresh the website.

How it works...

By calling `Loader::element`, we are actually injecting a partial template of PHP code into our theme. This code contains JavaScript and CSS files, as well as additional markup.

There's more...

Now that we have the edit bar visible, there are still no ways to add content to our simple theme. The next recipe will show how to add an editable area to the theme.

See also

▶ The *Creating a custom theme* recipe
▶ The *Defining editable content areas* recipe

Defining editable content areas

One great feature of concrete5's theme conventions is the ability to specify exactly where site editors are allowed to edit content. This prevents users from messing up the design and structure of the site, but still enables them to make edits to all the necessary content. In this recipe, we will add an editable area to the simple theme that we created earlier in the chapter.

Getting ready

We will expand on the theme created in the previous recipes. If you would like to catch up, the source code for this chapter is available for free on the book's website. You could also adapt this recipe to your own theme, if you'd like.

How to do it...

The steps for defining editable content areas are as follows:

1. Open `/themes/basic_theme/default.php` in your preferred code editor.
2. Replace the current `<h1>` tag with the following code:

```php
<?php $a = new Area('content'); $a->display($c); ?>
```

The screens will appear as shown in the following two screenshots:

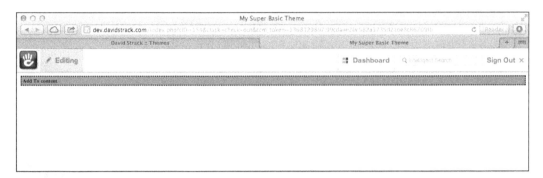

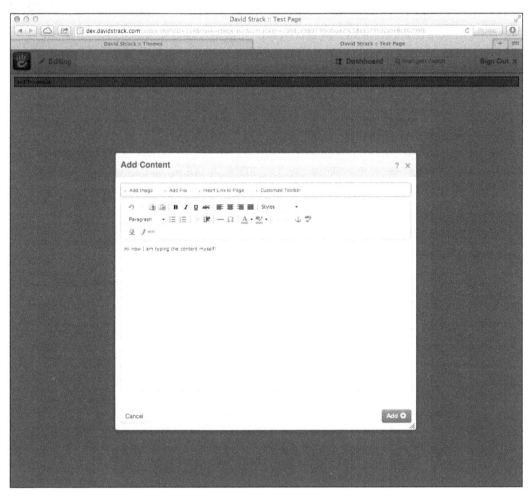

How it works...

The snippet of code that we added in this recipe essentially tells concrete5 that this is the place where blocks can be added.

There's more...

The snippet defining content areas can be placed anywhere in your site's HTML between the `<body>` tags. Imagine adding an area for the sidebar, and another area for the page's header. The only thing to note is that the name of the area (in this example, `content`) needs to be different in each place where it is used on a page.

See also

▸ The *Creating a custom theme* recipe
▸ The *Including the required concrete5 scripts and styles* recipe

Creating page type templates

concrete5 allows designers to create unlimited page templates for the pages in the website. These templates allow for different layouts, such as a sidebar, or may be a three-column layout. In this recipe, we will add a new page type template that shows a footer with a copyright statement to our existing basic theme.

Getting ready

We will be building upon the basic theme that was created in the first recipe of this chapter. The code for this chapter is freely available on the book's website, so feel free to download that for a starting point. Or, as always, you can adapt the recipe to fit your own website and theme's needs.

How to do it...

The steps for creating page type templates are as follows:

1. Create a new file in your theme directory (`/themes/basic_theme` for our current example) called `with_footer.php`.

2. Open the new file and paste the contents of `default.php`.

```
<!DOCTYPE html>
<html>
<head>
```

```
    <?php Loader::element('header_required') ?>
</head>
<body>
    <?php $a = new Area('content'); $a->display($c); ?>
    <?php Loader::element('footer_required') ?>
</body>
</html>
```

3. Add a footer to the page, displaying the copyright symbol, the current year, and the copyright holder.

```
<footer>
    &copy; <?php echo date('Y') ?> Somebody
</footer>
```

How it works...

concrete5 will use this template for all page types that have a handle of `with_footer`.

 If the page type has not been added through the concrete5 dashboard interface, this template cannot be used (page types can be added by visiting `/dashboard/pages/types`).

There's more...

Now, we have a new template, but we have violated one of the most important rules of programming: **don't repeat yourself** (**DRY**). We copied the complete HTML from the default template and pasted it into the new one. If something changes in the template and we want the change to be reflected on both of these templates, the developer would need to remember to update both the locations. The next recipe will cover the solution to this problem.

See also

▶ The *Creating a custom theme* recipe
▶ The *Using elements for repeating portions of HTML* recipe

Using elements for repeated portions of HTML

One of the fundamental rules for writing good code is summed up in the acronym, DRY. When creating themes, developers and designers will recognize that there are certain bits of code that get repeated on every page, such as a header or footer. In this recipe, we will learn how to use elements to safely repeat code between pages.

Getting ready

We are continuing to work on the very basic theme that was created in the first recipe of this chapter. The code for this chapter is available for free on the book's website if you'd like to use that as a starting point.

How to do it...

The steps for using elements for repeated portions of HTML are as follows:

1. Create a new directory in your `themes` folder called `elements`.

2. Create a new file in `elements/` called `header.php`.

3. Insert the following code into `header.php`:

```
<!DOCTYPE html>
<html>
<head>
  <?php Loader::element('header_required') ?>
</head>
<body>
```

4. Create a new file in `elements/` called `footer.php`.

5. Insert the following code into `footer.php`:

```
<?php Loader::element('footer_required') ?>
</body>
</html>
```

6. Open `default.php` from the `themes` directory.

7. Replace the header and footer code with the following code snippet, so that the entire file looks like the following:

```
<?php $this->inc('elements/header.php'); ?>
  <?php $a = new Area('content'); $a->display($c); ?>
<?php $this->inc('elements/footer.php'); ?>
```

8. Repeat the preceding steps for any page type templates that have been created.

How it works...

By storing the header and footer HTML in separate files, we can then tell concrete5 to include them in all of the templates that use them. This allows us to make edits to these elements in only one place and keep our template code clean.

See also

▸ The *Creating a custom theme* recipe

Customizing system pages

concrete5 makes it easy to create themes, but out of the box it does not apply themes to system pages, such as the login page. For most websites, this is fine, since only site editors will see the login page. On sites where site readers can log in and leave comments, or post in forums, it would be nice to have the login page match everything else. In this recipe, we will make the login page use the same theme as the rest of the site.

Getting ready

We will continue working with the custom theme that we built at the beginning of this chapter. As always, the code for this recipe is available to download for free from the website for this book.

How to do it...

The steps for customizing system pages are as follows:

1. Open `/config/site_theme_paths.php` in your preferred code editor.

2. Enter the following code in the `site_theme_paths.php` file:

    ```
    $v = View::getInstance();
    $v->setThemeByPath('/login', "basic_theme");
    ```

3. Open `/themes/basic_theme/view.php` in your code editor.

4. Enter the following code in `view.php`:

    ```
    <?php $this->inc('elements/header.php'); ?>
      <?php print $innerContent ?>
    <?php $this->inc('elements/footer.php'); ?>
    ```

How it works...

concrete5 comes with the `site_theme_paths.php` configuration file, but all of the configuration settings are commented out by default. This file lets you set the theme of any page on the site, and in this example, we tell it to use our basic theme for the login page.

You'll also notice that the `view.php` page was empty in our theme up until this point. This file is the template that concrete5 uses for single pages that do not have their own template defined. The `$innerContent` variable contains all of the PHP and HTML for the single page.

See also

▶   The *Creating a custom theme* recipe

Creating a custom add-on package

concrete5 allows developers to create modular components that can be reused and installed on any concrete5 website. These modules are called add-ons and are similar to plugins and modules in other content management systems. In this recipe, we will create a basic add-on that installs a single page to the concrete5 dashboard.

Getting ready

The complete code for this recipe is available for free from the book's website.

How to do it...

The steps for creating a custom add-on package are as follows:

1.   Create a new directory in `/packages` called `basic_addon`.

2.   Create a file called `controller.php` in `/packages/basic_addon`.

3.   Define the package class in `controller.php`.

    ```
    class BasicAddonPackage extends Package {}
    ```

4. Add the member variables to the class.

```
protected $pkgHandle = 'basic_addon';
protected $appVersionRequired = '5.5.0';
protected $pkgVersion = '1.0.0';
```

5. Define the function to return the package's name.

```
public function getPackageName() {
   return 'Basic Add-On';
}
```

6. Define a function to return the package's description.

```
public function getPackageDescription() {
   return 'This is a super-simple package';
}
```

7. Overwrite the `install` function, telling the package controller to also install a new single page on the dashboard.

```
public function install(){
   Loader::model('single_page');
   $pkg = parent::install();
   $page = SinglePage::add('/dashboard/hello', $pkg);
}
```

8. Create a directory in `basic_addon/` called `single_pages`.

9. Create a directory called `dashboard` in `single_pages/`.

10. Create a file called `hello.php` in /packages/basic_addon/single_pages/dashboard.

11. Enter the following code in `hello.php`.

```
<h1>Hello World!</h1>
```

12. In your web browser, visit the add-ons installation page in concrete5 at `/dashboard/extend/install/`. The page will look like the following screenshot:

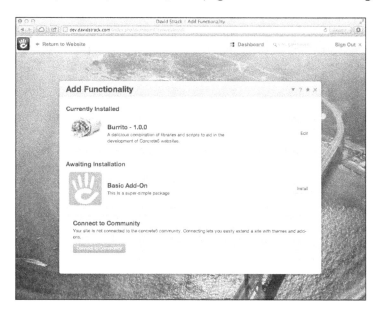

13. Click on the **Install** button by the new add-on that you have created.

14. Visit `/dashboard/hello` in your web browser to see the single page that got created by the package installer. The page will look like the following screenshot:

How it works...

The only required file in a package is `controller.php`. This file contains a class that provides methods for concrete5 to get the name and description of the add-on. We also modify the package installer by having it also add a new single page to the dashboard. By visiting `http://example.com/dashboard/hello`, we will see the HTML from the single page that we created.

There's more...

The structure of a package directory is very similar to the overall directory of a normal concrete5 site. Since we wanted to bundle a single page with our package, we simply had to create it and store it in a directory much like we would normally in concrete5. You can see how a package would be structured if it had to contain blocks, controllers, helpers, or any other type of file that concrete5 uses.

See also

  ▸   The *Using the package controller to execute custom code* recipe

Using the package controller to execute custom code

A unique and advanced feature of the package controller is the ability to run code automatically whenever a page is accessed. This can give add-on developers tremendous potential to tap into system events, hook into site HTTP requests, and more. In this recipe, we will show how easy it is to automatically run code from our package whenever a page is visited by redirecting all requests containing a special parameter to the home page.

Getting ready

We will use the simple add-on package that was created in the previous recipe for this example. The code for this recipe and all others is available for download on the book's website.

How to do it...

The steps for using the package controller to execute custom code are as follows:

  1.   Open the package controller file, located at `/packages/basic_addon/controller.php`.

2. Add a function called `on_start` that will redirect anyone that enters the parameter `redirect_me` in the URL.

```
public function on_start() {
if (isset($_GET['redirect_me'])) {
    header('Location: /');
  }
}
```

3. Test it out by adding `?redirect_me` to the URL.

How it works...

concrete5 automatically runs the function `on_start` whenever a page is loaded, so any code that you place there in your package will get automatically run. Our example in this case is pretty useless, but you can see where the opportunities are nearly endless for developers (automatically parsing page requests, intercepting form submissions, adding CSS or JavaScript to pages, and more).

See also

▶ The *Creating a custom add-on package* recipe

9
System Events and Advanced Configuration

In this chapter we will cover the following recipes:

- ▶ Declaring advanced configuration variables
- ▶ Enabling events in concrete5
- ▶ Listening to system events
- ▶ Passing parameters to event handlers
- ▶ Defining a page type event
- ▶ Sending an e-mail when a user creates an account
- ▶ Sending an e-mail when a file has been uploaded
- ▶ Creating a custom scheduled job
- ▶ Making your add-on translation ready
- ▶ Rebranding concrete5 as a white label CMS
- ▶ Changing the dashboard background image

Introduction

concrete5 contains a lot of miscellaneous advanced functionality for developers. Earlier in the book, we have touched on the concept of events in concrete5. In this chapter, we will explore recipes to listen for system events and act upon them, as well as create customized configuration settings and even change the concrete5 branding to white label the CMS as your own.

About the code in this chapter

This chapter will sometimes place code in places, such as `/config/site_post.php`, which can sometimes interrupt the normal operation of the website. Make sure you perform these recipes on a development server!

Declaring advanced configuration variables

concrete5 comes with a bunch of "secret" advanced configuration variables that developers can set to augment the behavior of concrete5. In this recipe, we will set a hypothetical configuration setting.

How to do it...

The steps for declaring advanced configuration variables are as follows:

1. Open the site configuration file, located at `/config/site.php` in your preferred code editor.

2. Declare a new constant variable called `FOO` and set its value to `BAR`, as follows:

   ```
   define('FOO', 'BAR');
   ```

3. Save the `site.php` file.

How it works...

concrete5 simply loads this file at the beginning of every page request. By defining configuration settings here, developers can override default concrete5 settings and also create their own constant variables. If a developer were to dump the contents of the constant `FOO`, they would see the string `BAR`.

Enabling events in concrete5

concrete5 comes with a publish/subscribe event model that makes it easy for developers to have their code respond to system events. If developers wish to declare events in `/config/site_events.php` (which we do in this chapter), they must be enabled in `site.php`.

How to do it...

The steps to enable events are as follows:

1. Locate the file `/config/site.php` and open it in your preferred code editor.
2. Add the following configuration setting to `config.php`:

   `define('ENABLE_APPLICATION_EVENTS', true);`

3. Save the file.
4. Clear the concrete5 cache by visiting `/dashboard/system/optimization/clear_cache/` and clicking on the **Clear Cache** button.

How it works...

Before concrete5 allows developers to register event listeners in `/config/site_events.php`, it will check to see if this configuration setting is present and set to `true`.

There's more...

In later concrete5 versions (Versions 5.5 and above) this step can be ignored, though this author's personal preference is to put the configuration in place anyway, so that events can be enabled or disabled (by setting the value to `false`) with ease.

See also

- ► The *Declaring advanced configuration variables* recipe
- ► The *Listening to system events* recipe

Listening to system events

Once events have been enabled in concrete5, developers can write their own code to respond to the different events. In this recipe, we will create a basic "Hello World!" event that runs immediately when a page is visited and outputs a message to the screen.

Getting ready

Before you can register an event in `site_events.php`, concrete5 must be configured to enable the events system. Refer to the previous recipe to see how to enable events.

How to do it...

The steps are as follows:

1. Create a new file in `/config` called `site_events.php`.

2. Open `site_events.php` in your preferred code editor.

3. Add the following code to listen to the `on_start` event.

   ```
   Events::extend('on_start', 'MyClass', 'onStartFired', 'libraries/
   my_class.php');
   ```

4. Create a new file in `/libraries` called `my_class.php`.

5. Define a new class called `MyClass` in `my_class.php`.

   ```
   class MyClass {
   }
   ```

6. Add a method to `MyClass` called `onStartFired`.

   ```
   public function onStartFired() {
   }
   ```

7. In `onStartFired`, use the `die` function to output **hello world!**.

   ```
   die('hello world!');
   ```

8. Visit any page on your site. You will see a white screen with the words **hello world!** as shown in the following screenshot:

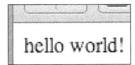

9. Feel free to comment out the `die` statement in the `onStartFired` function of `MyClass` to restore your site to proper working order.

How it works...

concrete5 will automatically check for the presence of the `/config/site_events.php` file and execute any code contained within it while the site is loading (much like how `/config/site_post.php` behaves). This is the perfect place to experiment with our event registrations. When we call `Event::extend()`, we pass in arguments that specify which event we want to listen to, the class name that our event handler resides in (`MyClass`, in this example), the method within that class that will be executed when the event is fired (`onStartFired`, in this case), and finally the path to the file containing our handler class.

See also

▸ The *Enabling events in concrete5* recipe

▸ The *Passing parameters to event handlers* recipe

Passing parameters to event handlers

Event handlers are the functions that concrete5 executes when events are fired. In the previous recipe, we used the custom class `MyClass` and its function `onStartFired` as the event handler. concrete5 allows developers to actually pass parameters to these handlers as well. In this recipe, we build upon the event handler from the previous recipe and pass a message to the `onStartFired` handler, which will output that message.

Getting ready

We will be using the code that we created in the previous recipe as the base for this one. Also, make sure that you have enabled events as described in the first recipe in this chapter.

How to do it...

The steps for passing parameters to event handlers are as follows:

1. Open the `site_events.php` file located in `/config` in your code editor.

2. Add a new argument to the event registration code, so it looks like the following code:

   ```
   Events::extend('on_start', 'MyClass', 'onStartFired', 'libraries/
   my_class.php', array('This is a custom message!'));
   ```

3. Open `/libraries/my_class.php` and change `onStartFired` so that it looks like the following code:

   ```
   public function onStartFired($view, $message) {
     die($message);
   }
   ```

4. You will now be able to see the new message when you refresh your website as shown in the following screenshot:

5. Feel free to comment out the `die` statement to allow your site to function as normal.

How it works...

By adding a fifth parameter to the `Events::extend()` function call, we can send parameters to the event handler function. This new parameter needs to be an array, which contains the various parameters that we wish to send to the handler.

You may notice that our handler function, `onStartFired`, has two parameters (`$view` and `$message`), when we only specified the message parameter. This is because concrete5 provides the current `View` object to the handler as a bit of context, which can be useful. If you are ever unsure of which parameters have been applied to your function, dump the result of the `func_get_args()` function of PHP to see an array of all of the parameters that have been sent, as they can vary between events.

See also

- ▸ The *Enabling events in concrete5* recipe
- ▸ The *Listening to system events* recipe

Defining a page type event

In addition to providing a variety of events that developers can hook into, concrete5 also provides an events system at the page type level. We discussed page types in detail in the first chapter of this book, but now we can add a custom event to our page types. In this recipe, we will create a page type called `blog_post` and hook into the `on_page_add` event for that page type.

Getting ready

Page types and how to work with them are described in much more detail in *Chapter 1, Pages and Page Types*. Make sure events are enabled in concrete5 and that your `/config/site_events.php` file exists.

How to do it...

The steps for defining a page type event are as follows:

1. Register the event handler in `/config/site_events.php`:

   ```
   Events::extendPageType('blog_post', 'on_page_add');
   ```

2. First, create a new page type file in `/page_types` called `blog_post.php`.

3. Next, create the controller file for the page type in `/controllers/page_types/blog_post.php`.

4. Create the controller class, extending the core `Controller` class:

```
class BlogPostPageTypeController extends Controller {
}
```

5. Add a method to the controller class called `on_page_add`:

```
public function on_page_add() {
}
```

6. In the `on_page_add` function, create a simple `die` statement so we know that this event is working:

```
die('blog post added');
```

7. Install the page type by visiting `/dashboard/pages/types`.

8. Click on **Add a Page Type**.

9. Give the page type a name and make sure the handle is set to `blog_post`.

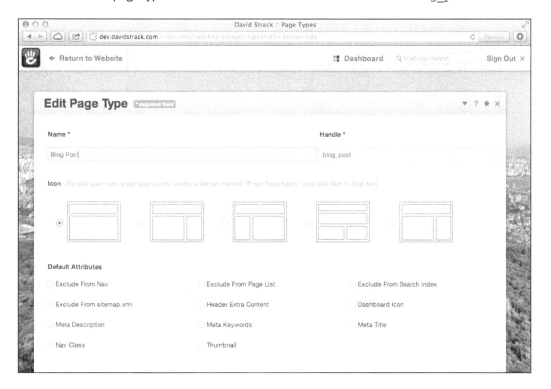

10. Now visit the sitemap, located at `/dashboard/sitemap/full/`.

11. Add a new page to the site, choose blog post as the page type.

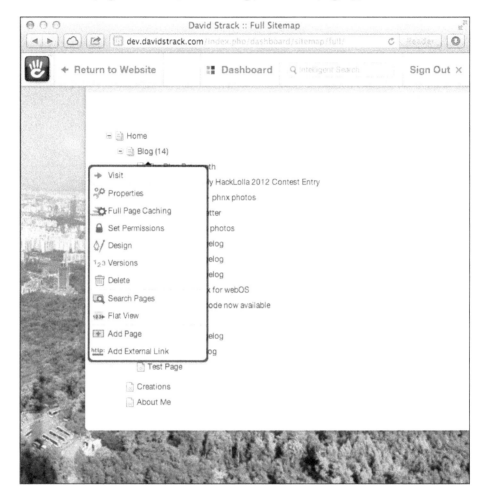

12. Add a blog post as shown in the following screenshot:

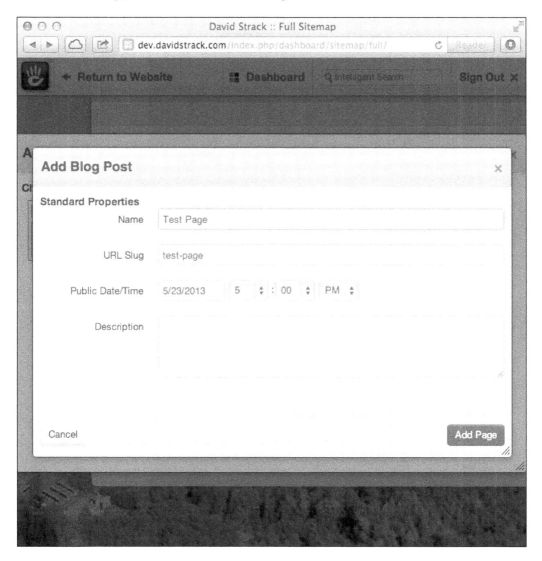

13. When the page is added, you will see the message that you created in the event handler, as shown in the following screenshot:

14. Don't forget to remove the `die` statement from your event handler so that your website returns to normal functionality.

How it works...

When adding events to page types, concrete5 removes the need for developers to manually specify the class name, function name, and file location of the event handler. Because page types follow a specific convention (the controller name is called `BlogPostPageTypeController`) and are usually located in the `/controllers/page_types` directory, concrete5 can automatically determine which file and class should be loaded to handle the event.

There's more...

Parameters can be passed to page type event handlers just like they are in regular event handlers. Simply add a third parameter to the event declaration, an array containing each of the parameters to be passed onto the handler function as follows:

```
Events::extendPageType('blog_post', 'on_page_add', array('This is a custom parameter'));
```

The new parameter can then be accessed from the handler function:

```
public function on_page_add($view, $message) {
    die($message);
}
```

See also

- ▶ The *Enabling events in concrete5* recipe
- ▶ The *Listening to system events* recipe
- ▶ The *Passing parameters to event handlers* recipe

Sending an e-mail when a user creates an account

We have covered a number of recipes pertaining to events in concrete5 so far in this chapter. Now we can try out a common real-world example of using system events to execute custom code. In this recipe, we will send an e-mail to a site administrator whenever a user registers on the website.

Getting ready

Sending e-mails can be tricky business in PHP, as a lot of it can depend on individual server configuration. We will be using concrete5's Mail helper (discussed in more detail in *Chapter 4*, Using the *Core Helpers*), which helps a little bit, but misconfigured servers can still have problems. We will assume that your server (development or otherwise) is capable of sending e-mails.

Also, make sure that events are enabled in concrete5 as described in the *Declaring advanced configuration variables* recipe of this chapter!

How to do it...

The steps for sending an e-mail when a user creates an account, are as follows:

1. Declare the event listener in `/config/site_events.php`:

   ```
   Events::extend('on_user_add', 'UserEmailer', 'newAccountCreated',
   'libraries/user_emailer.php');
   ```

2. Create the `user_emailer.php` file mentioned in the event registration in /libraries:

3. Define a new class in `user_emailer.php` called `UserEmailer`:

   ```
   class UserEmailer {
   }
   ```

4. Add a method to `UserEmailer` called `newAccountCreated`, which accepts one parameter, a `UserInfo` object called `$user`:

   ```
   public function newAccountCreated($user) {
   }
   ```

5. In the `newAccountCreated` function, load the Mail helper:

   ```
   $mail = Loader::helper('mail');
   ```

6. Set the subject of the e-mail:

   ```
   $mail->setSubject('New account created!');
   ```

7. Set the body of the e-mail:

```
$mail->setBody('Someone with the email address of '.$user-
>uEmail.' has created an account.');
```

8. Set the destination address of the e-mail (set this to an e-mail that you own, so you can make sure that it works):

```
$mail->to('somebody@example.com');
```

9. Set the `from` address to something appropriate for your own website:

```
$mail->from('noreply@example.com');
```

10. Send the e-mail:

```
$mail->sendMail();
```

11. Test that this event works by adding a new user to your website.

12. Visit `/dashboard/users/add/` of your concrete5 website to add a new user.

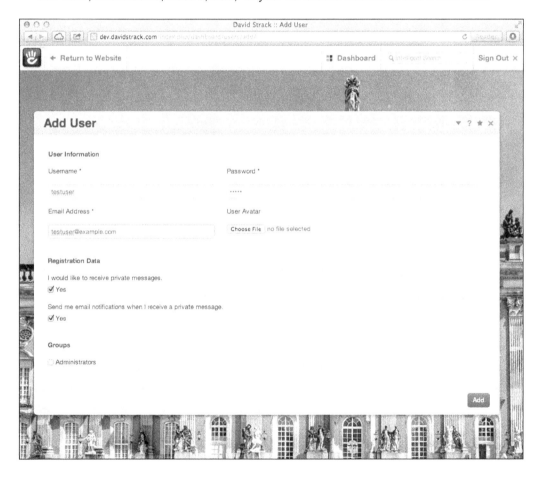

13. Once the user has been added, you should receive an e-mail.

How it works...

When the event listener gets defined in `site_events.php`, concrete5 will remember to execute the provided function when the relevant event is fired. In this case, concrete5 fires the `on_user_add` event once a new user is added to the database, thereby running our custom code that we created. Using the Mail helper, we are able to programmatically generate an e-mail and send it immediately.

See also

▶ The *Sending e-mails with the Mail helper* recipe in *Chapter 4, Using the Core Helpers*

▶ The *Listening to system events* recipe

Sending an e-mail when a file has been uploaded

We are going to play around with sending e-mails again; this time we will send someone an e-mail whenever a file gets added to the file manager. The e-mail will contain a link to download the file.

How to do it...

The steps for sending an e-mail when a file has been uploaded, are as follows:

1. Set up the event listener in `/config/site_events.php`:

```
Events::extend('on_file_add', 'FileEmailer', 'fileUploaded',
'libraries/file_emailer.php');
```

2. Create a new library in `/libraries/file_emailer.php`:

3. Declare the new `FileEmailer` class:

```
class FileEmailer {
}
```

4. Add a method to the class called `fileUploaded`:

```
public function fileUploaded($file, $fv) {
}
```

5. Load the Mail helper:

```
$mail = Loader::helper('mail');
```

6. Set the subject of the message:

```
$mail->setSubject('A file has been added to the file manager');
```

7. Set the body of the message, including a link to download the file:

```
$mail->setBody('A new file has been uploaded. Download it here: '.
  $fv->getDownloadURL());
```

8. Add the recipient's e-mail address (change this to an e-mail address that you have access to):

```
$mail->to('somebody@example.com');
```

9. Set the return address:

```
$mail->from('noreply@example.com');
```

10. Send the e-mail:

```
$mail->sendMail();
```

11. Visit your website's file manager at `/dashboard/files/search`.

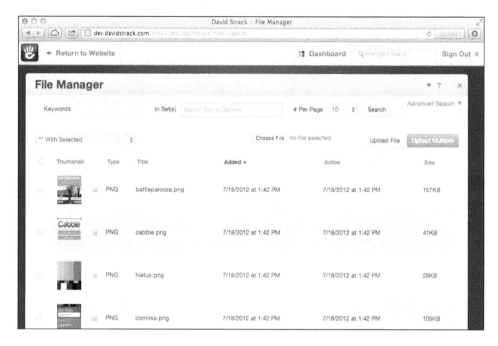

12. Upload a new file.
13. You will receive an e-mail containing a link to download the new file as shown in the following screenshot:

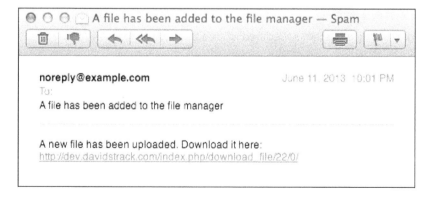

How it works...

When a file gets uploaded, concrete5 automatically fires off the `on_file_add` event, which we registered a listener for in `/config/site_events.php`. concrete5 passes `File` and `FileVersion` objects as the two parameters in the event callback. The `FileVersion` object contains the method to get the download URL.

See also

▸ The *Sending an e-mail when a user creates an account* recipe

Creating a custom scheduled job

concrete5 allows developers to create special jobs to run automatically via scheduled tasks on the server. These jobs can be any sort of action that you wish to perform automatically on a regular basis. In this recipe, we will write a job that will send a good morning e-mail to every user on the website.

Getting ready

It probably should go without saying, but please make sure to perform this recipe on a test server with test users and e-mail addresses. You don't want to annoy your entire user base with silly e-mails every morning.

How to do it...

The steps for creating a custom scheduled job are as follows:

1. Create a new file at `/jobs/email_everyone.php`.

2. Declare a new class called `EmailEveryone`:
   ```
   class EmailEveryone extends Job {
   }
   ```

3. Create a method in the class to return the job's name:
   ```
   public function getJobName() {
     return 'Wakeup Email';
   }
   ```

4. Create another method to return the job's description:
   ```
   public function getJobDescription() {
     return 'Give all of your site members a morning wakeup email!';
   }
   ```

5. Create a function called `run`:

```
public function run() {
}
```

6. Load the `UserList` model:

```
Loader::model('user_list');
```

7. Create a new instance of the `UserList` class:

```
$ul = new UserList();
```

8. Get an array of all of the users on the website:

```
$users = $ul->get();
```

9. Loop through the array:

```
foreach ($users as $user) {
}
```

10. In the loop, load the Mail helper:

```
$mail = Loader::helper('mail');
```

11. Set the subject of the e-mail:

```
$mail->setSubject('Good morning!');
```

12. Set the reply address:

```
$mail->from('noreply@example.com');
```

13. Set the destination address to the current user in the loop:

```
$mail->to($user->getUserEmail());
```

14. Set the body of the e-mail, including the user's username:

```
$mail->setBody('Good morning, '.$user->getUserName());
```

15. Send the e-mail:

```
$mail->sendMail();
```

16. Return a message to display on the dashboard:

```
return 'Emailed '.count($users).' users.';
```

17. Visit the **Automated Jobs** page of the dashboard, located at `/dashboard/system/optimization/jobs/`.

18. You will see your new job at the bottom of the list as shown in the following screenshot.

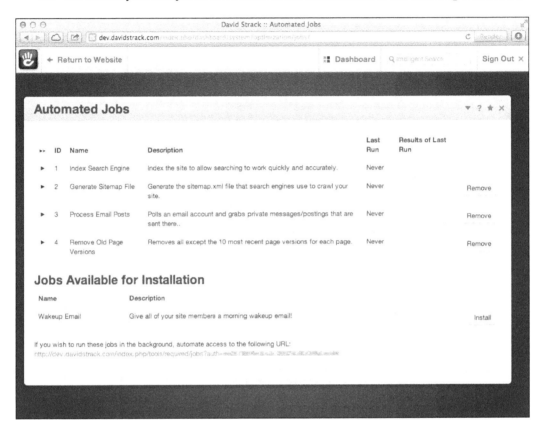

19. Click on the **Install** button as shown in the preceding screenshot.

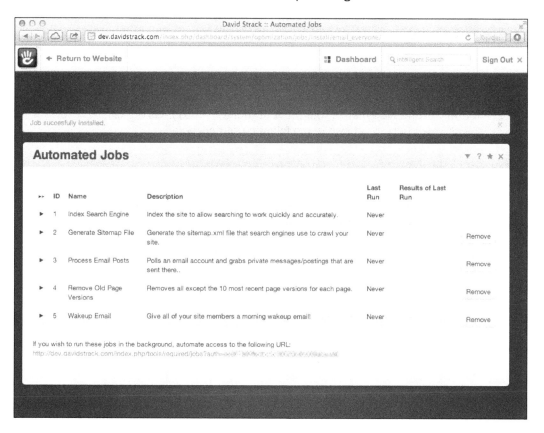

20. Click on the triangle play icon to run your job. You will see a message showing how many users were mailed.

21. You will receive an e-mail in your inbox (if your e-mail address is assigned to one of the site members) as shown in the following screenshot:

How it works...

concrete5 will asynchronously run the new task once the "play" button is clicked. The task simply loads a list of all of the users on the site, and e-mails each of them. In production use, this is inefficient for a large amount of members and can even get your server blacklisted for spam.

There's more...

You may be wondering how to automatically run something like this. The answer lies within server automated tasks. On most Linux web servers, site administrators will use the `cron` scheduler to manage automatic tasks, and possibly the `curl` command to send an HTTP request to the task runner. To run this task automatically, create a scheduled task to ping the URL listed at the bottom of the jobs page. This URL contains a token that will allow your system to access concrete5 without logging in. Make sure to keep this URL and its token private, otherwise unauthorized users could trigger your site's automated tasks.

For more information on creating scheduled tasks on your Linux-based web server, see `https://en.wikipedia.org/wiki/Cron`.

Making your add-on translation ready

concrete5 allows developers to take advanced steps to make sure that their code is compatible with concrete5 translations. In this recipe, we will show how to prepare a string for translation.

How to do it...

The steps for making add-on translation ready are as follows:

1. Open `/config/site_post.php` in your code editor.
2. Declare a string for testing:

```
$str = 'Hello world!';
```

3. Use the translation function to output your string:

```
echo t($str);
exit;
```

How it works...

concrete5 makes use of the Zend translation library. concrete5 defines the global `t()` function as a shortcut to make strings available to various translations. Translators then will prepare translation files using a tool such as Poedit to assist with translating these strings. To learn more about Poedit and creating translation files, see `http://www.poedit.net`.

Rebranding concrete5 as a white label CMS

concrete5 allows developers to change the logo, title, and general branding information of the CMS to whatever they would prefer. Often larger organizations like to white label their products like this, and concrete5 makes it easy. In this recipe, we will white label concrete5 by changing the logo in the edit bar.

Getting ready

You will need an image of your logo that is 49 x 49 pixels. We are using a sample logo in this recipe, which is included with the code download from this book's website.

How to do it...

The steps are as follows:

1. Upload your new logo to your site. In this example, our logo is located at `/images/new-logo.png` (you may need to create the images directory)

2. Open `/config/site.php` in your code editor.

3. Add the following configuration to the file:

   ```
   define('WHITE_LABEL_LOGO_SRC', '/images/new-logo.png');
   ```

4. Save the file. You will now see the new logo in the edit bar as shown in the following screenshot:

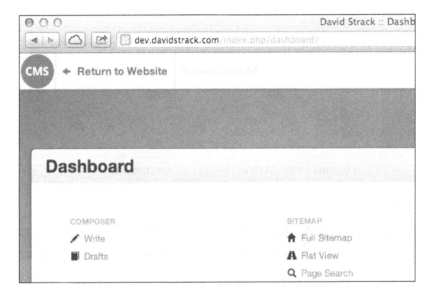

How it works...

concrete5 checks for the presence of this configuration variable and changes the logo source if that is present. concrete5 will also add a **Powered by concrete5** message to the edit bar if the logo has been changed.

There's more...

There are a few more white labeling aspects that are available for developers. There is a great list available at `http://www.concrete5.org/documentation/how-tos/developers/white-labelling/`.

See also

▸ The *Declaring advanced configuration variables* recipe

Changing the dashboard background image

By default, concrete5 displays big and bright photographs in the background of every dashboard page. These images are powered by a feed running on concrete5's official servers, and the image changes every day.

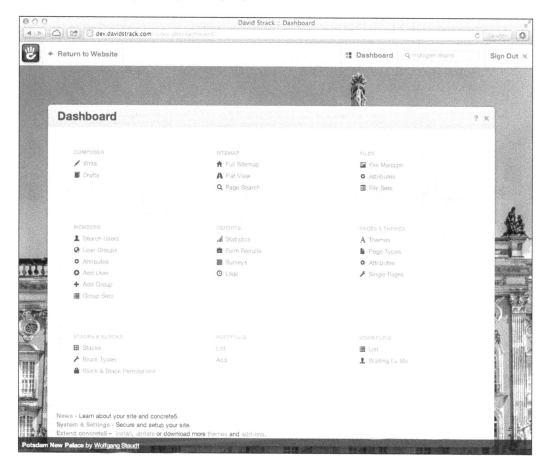

It's a fun effect and brings a lot of color into the dashboard, but some clients and agencies might not like showing random photos on their site, especially if it is used for business. Fortunately, concrete5 makes it easy to change the background image.

Getting ready

You will need a new image to use for the background, with a size of at least 1024 x 768 pixels. In this example, we will be using a subtle dark gradient that can be quickly created in Adobe Photoshop, but you can use any image you like. The background image is available with the code download of this book.

How to do it...

The steps for changing the background image of dashboard are as follows:

1. Open the `/config/site.php` file in your code editor.

2. Add the following configuration to the file.

   ```
   define('WHITE_LABEL_DASHBOARD_BACKGROUND_SRC', '/images/new-
   background.png');
   ```

3. Save the file. The background of the dashboard will now be changed.

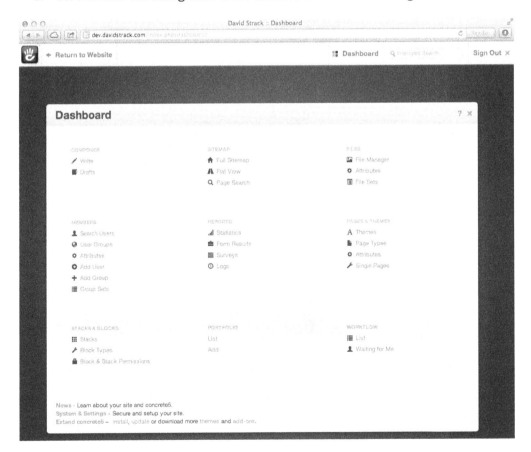

How it works...

concrete5 simply checks for the `WHITE_LABEL_DASHBOARD_BACKGROUND_SRC` configuration setting and replaces the daily image with the new background that you have provided.

There's more...

Developers can get rid of the background picture entirely by setting the background source to "none".

See also

- ▸ The *Declaring advanced configuration variables* recipe.

Blueprint – Creating an Image Gallery Add-on

Now that we have learned dozens of concrete5 recipes, it is time to put them to practical use. Think of this chapter as one giant recipe, with the sole purpose of creating an image gallery add-on, which you can install on your concrete5 website and begin using right away. If you visit the website for this book, there is a complete download of the source code to help you out if you get stuck.

Before we begin...

This entire chapter was developed with a fresh installation of concrete5 Version 5.6.1.2, though the code will technically work for any concrete5 after Version 5.6. If you'd like to follow along exactly, get a new version of concrete5 running on your development server and install the sample content with it. That will give us some pages and images to work with.

Creating the package controller

The first step in creating our add-on is to create the directories and files.

Create a new directory in /packages called cookbook_gallery. The first file we will need is controller.php.

Enter the following code in controller.php to define the add-on:

```php
<?php
defined('C5_EXECUTE') or die(_("Access Denied."));

class CookbookGalleryPackage extends Package {
```

```
protected $pkgHandle = 'cookbook_gallery';

protected $appVersionRequired = '5.6.0';

protected $pkgVersion = '0.9.0';

public function getPackageName() {
  return t('Cookbook Gallery');
}

public function getPackageDescription() {
   return t('An image gallery that ties into the file manager.');
}

}
```

You may recall from *Chapter 8, Working with Themes and Add-Ons*, that packages only require one file, the `controller`. The `controller` file contains methods that tell concrete5 what the package's name is, and a text description of the package.

There are a few things we need to make note of here. First, notice the class name of the controller. Since our package handle is `cookbook_gallery`, we need to camel case that handle and append the package to the end, to create the class name that concrete5 can predict and load correctly.

The next thing we need is the `defined` or `die` statement at the top of the file. This is a special security requirement of concrete5 to ensure that scripts cannot be executed arbitrarily. Everything has to get run through the concrete5 dispatcher. This statement is required at the top of every `.php` (excluding third-party libraries that exist in `libraries/3rd_party`) file in your package if you plan on submitting the package to the concrete5 marketplace.

Another thing that we need to pay attention to is that all public facing strings are encased in the `t()` function (see the package name and description). The `t()` function, as discussed in *Chapter 9, System Events and Advanced Configuration* allows translators to supply alternate translations for the given string. This is another requirement for add-ons to be submitted into the concrete5 marketplace.

We aren't done with the controller yet; we will need to come back and add the installation function once our block is created.

Creating the block type

Our image gallery is going to be a custom block type. This block type can be added to any page in the concrete5 site, and will show an image gallery wherever it is placed. The first thing we will need to do is create the block's directory. Add a new directory in `/packages/cookbook_gallery/blocks`. Inside the new block's directory, add a directory called `cookbook_gallery`. This will contain our block's files.

The block's controller

First up for our block type is the `controller` file. Create `controller.php` in `/packages/cookbook_gallery_blocks/cookbook_gallery`.

Declare the block `controller` class and add the following methods:

```php
<?php defined('C5_EXECUTE') or die(_("Access Denied."));

class CookbookGalleryBlockController extends BlockController {

  protected $btTable = "btCookbookGallery";
  protected $btInterfaceWidth = "350";
  protected $btInterfaceHeight = "300";

  var $defaultCount = 20;

  public function getBlockTypeName() {
    return t('Photo Gallery');
  }

  public function getBlockTypeDescription() {
    return t('Shows photos from a file set.');
  }

}
```

Again, notice the `defined` or `die` statement at the top of the file and the use of `t()` functions to wrap our public facing strings. We have also defined the name of the block's database table, using the member variable `$btTable`.

Save the `controller` file, we will be coming back to it later to add our block's functionality.

The database XML file

The next file that our block type needs is the database XML file. Create it at `/packages/cookbook_gallery/blocks/cookbook_gallery/db.xml`. This file defines all of the tables and fields that the block type will need. concrete5 will automatically create the defined tables when the block type is installed.

You may recall from *Chapter 2, Working with Blocks* that this file makes use of ADOdb's XML schema (or AXMLS). You can learn more about AXMLS on the ADOdb website, located at `http://phplens.com/lens/adodb/docs-datadict.htm#xmlschema`.

Enter the following XML code in `db.xml`:

```
<?xml version="1.0"?>
<schema version="0.3">
  <table name="btCookbookGallery">
    <field name="bID" type="I">
      <key />
      <unsigned />
    </field>
    <field name="file_set" type="I"></field>
    <field name="count" type="I"></field>
  </table>
</schema>
```

We created a database table with the same name that we specified in the block type's controller. The table has two fields, a unique integer ID called `bID` (which is required for the block to be installed), and an integer file set ID field. Save this `db.xml` file, and you can close it if you'd like, as we won't be needing it again.

The block type's view files

Finally, we will need to create files for the various views for the block. The block has three views—add, edit, and view. Create `add.php`, `edit.php`, and `view.php` in the block's directory. Since add and edit share the same HTML, we will create a shared template that both views will include, called `form.php`. Oh, why not create `view.css` as well, since our view file will need to use some styles.

The resulting contents of our new package are in the following screenshot:

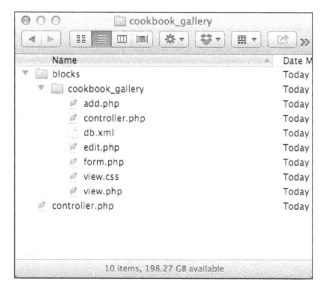

Let's leave these view files empty for now, because we want to install our block type and its package to the website!

Installing the block type with the package

Right now, if we were to install the package, the block type would not come with it, and users of your add-on would be confused and disappointed. We can tell the package to install the block type during the package's installation, though.

Open the package `controller` (`/packages/cookbook_gallery/controller.php`) in your code editor.

Add a new method to the `controller` class called `install`, as follows:

```
public function install() {
  $pkg = parent::install();

  // install the block type
  BlockType::installBlockTypeFromPackage('cookbook_gallery', $pkg);
}
```

What's going on here? Well, the `Package` class has a function called `install`, which, you guessed it, installs the package to the concrete5 database. Since our package controller extends the `Package` class, the `install` function is automatically available to us.

The first step is to call the `Package` class's `install` function and get the object that it returns. This will allow us to install the block type and have it assigned to our package.

It's important to pass the `$pkg` object to the block type installer, because if users uninstall or reinstall your add-on, the block type will come and go with it.

Save the controller file. It's time to install our add-on!

Installing the package in concrete5

Visit `/dashboard/extend/install/` on your concrete5 site (you'll have to log in if your haven't already). You will see your add-on awaiting installation.

The gallery add-on awaiting installation is as shown in the following screenshot:

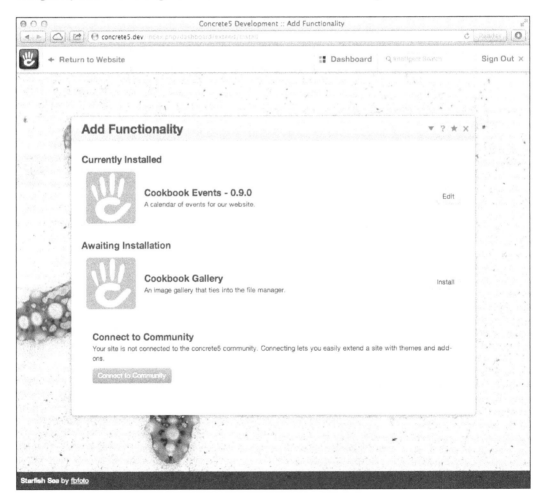

Click on the **Install** button. concrete5 will add your package and its block controller to the site. If it succeeds, you will see a message at the top of the screen.

After successful installation of the add-on, we see the following screenshot:

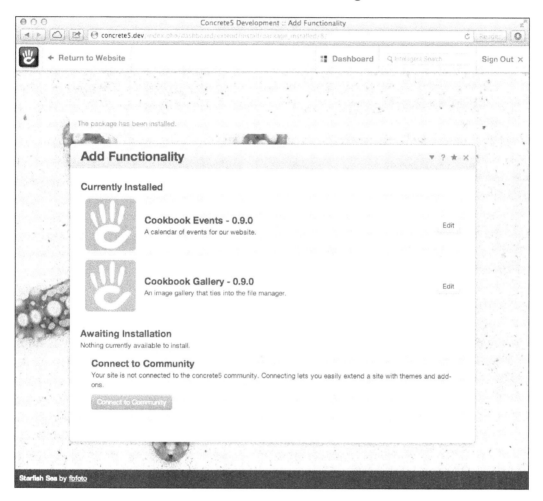

Creating a page for the gallery

Visit your concrete5 homepage and hover over the **Edit** button to add a sub-page underneath the home page.

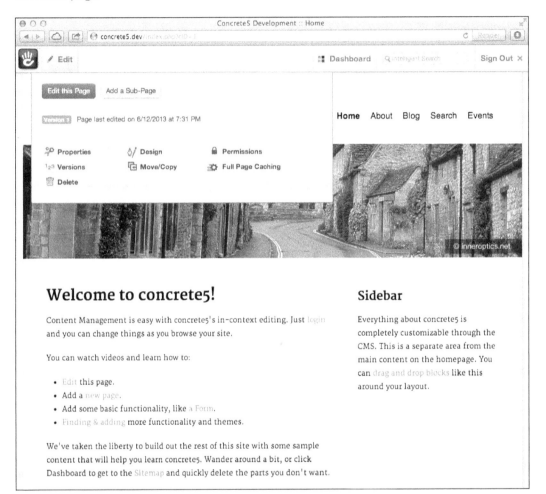

Let's use the **Full** layout for this gallery page.

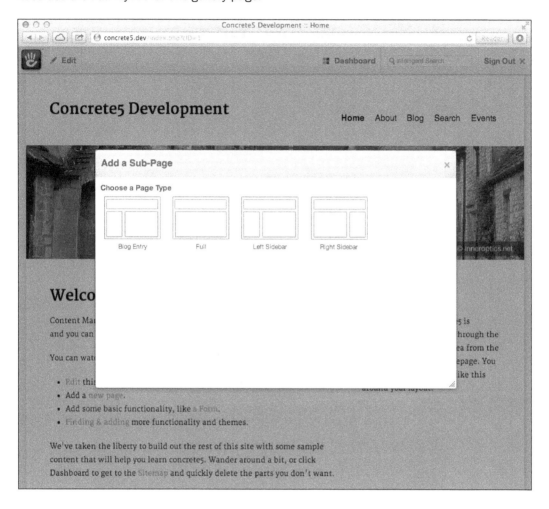

Give the page a title and path. How about `Image Gallery`?

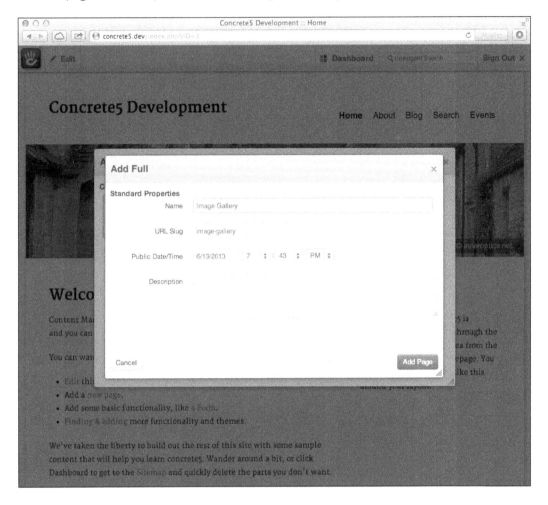

Add the page to the site. Now that we have a nice place to put our block, let's actually make our block do something!

Giving life to the block

Open your block's controller (located at `/packages/cookbook_gallery/blocks/ cookbook_gallery/controller.php`) in your code editor. We need to add some functions to this class to make it work. First, let's bring the block's add and edit forms to life. Add the following functions to the `controller` class.

```
public function add() {
  $this->addEdit();
```

```
  }

  public function edit() {
    $this->addEdit();
  }

  public function addEdit() {
    $fsList = new FileSetList();
    $sets = $fsList->get();

    $options = array();

    foreach ($sets as $fs) {
      $options[$fs->fsID] = $fs->fsName;
    }

    $this->set('sets', $options);
  }
```

Whoa, what are we doing here? You may recall from earlier chapters that concrete5 controllers employ the use of callbacks, which are functions in the class that get automatically executed when certain things happen. Whenever a block is added to a page for the first time, concrete5 will call the add function when the add.php view is displayed. The same goes for the edit function and the edit.php view.

Since we want the same code to run when both add and edit forms are used, why not create a function that they each can use? The addEdit function contains the real code for our backend work.

First, we load a list of all of the file sets in the concrete5 database. Next, we transform this list of file sets into a simple key/value array that we can feed into a select box in the HTML form. Lastly, we send the array of <select> options to the view as the variable $sets.

Awesome. Now, what about when the gallery block is actually viewed on the website? There's a callback for that, too.

```
  public function view() {
    if ($this->file_set) {
      $list = new FileList();
      $set = FileSet::getByID($this->file_set);

      $list->filterBySet($set);
      $list->filterByType(FileType::T_IMAGE);

      $count = ($this->count) ? $this->count : $this->defaultCount;

      $this->set('images', $list->get($count));
```

```
    }
    else {
      $this->set('images', false);
    }
  }
```

The `view` function will be automatically run by concrete5 whenever the block is displayed on the website. It is here that we load the images from the chosen file set and send them to the view.

First, we need to create a new instance of the `FileList` class. This class allows us to filter the files in the file manager, to only show the ones that belong in our image gallery.

Next, we load the file set object, based on the file set ID that we will set in the add/edit form. Using the file set object, we are able to filter the set to only show us files that are in that set. We don't want all types of files appearing though (imagine a PDF in the image gallery—that's no fun!), so we add another filter to only show us images.

Next, we write a ternary expression to fall back on the default gallery limit, if one was not chosen when the block was added to the page.

Finally, let's send the images array to the view, so we can show our gallery!

Filling out the add and edit view files

Alright, so we have some great code in our controller, but there's still no HTML in our views. Let's fix that right now.

Open `form.php` in your code editor. We are going to create the HTML form that site editors will see when the block is added or edited on a page.

Enter the following HTML and PHP code in `form.php`:

```php
<?php
defined('C5_EXECUTE') or die(_("Access Denied."));
$form = Loader::helper('form');
?>

<div class="ccm-ui">
  <table class="table table-striped table-bordered">
    <tr>
      <td>
        <?php echo t('File set to show photos from') ?>
      </td>
      <td>
        <?php echo $form->select('file_set', $sets, $file_set) ?>
      </td>
```

```
        </tr>
        <tr>
          <td>
            <?php echo t('How many images to show?') ?>
          </td>
          <td>
            <?php echo $form->text('count', $count) ?>
          </td>
        </tr>
      </table>
    </div>
```

Hey, that wasn't so bad! This form will contain two fields—a select box containing a list of the file sets in concrete5, and a text input to limit the image gallery. Don't worry about wrapping it in a form element or adding save controls, concrete5 will take care of all of that.

Now, let's include this form in `add.php` and `edit.php`. Add the following code to both files:

```
<?php
defined('C5_EXECUTE') or die(_("Access Denied."));
  $this->inc('form.php');
```

That's it! Now when our block gets added to the website, editors will see our nice new form.

Creating the gallery view file

Of course, our gallery is still missing the most important component, the gallery itself. Let's add some HTML and PHP to `view.php` to show the various images in the chosen file set as follows:

```
<?php
  defined('C5_EXECUTE') or die(_("Access Denied."));
  $ih = Loader::helper('image');
?>

<h1><?php echo t('Image Gallery') ?></h1>

<?php if ($images !== false): ?>
  <div class="gallery-wrapper">
    <?php foreach ($images as $image): ?>
      <?php $thumbnail = $ih->getThumbnail($image, 100, 100, true); ?>
      <a class="gallery-image" href="<?php echo $image->getRelativePath() ?>">
        <img src="<?php echo $thumbnail->src ?>" />
      </a>
    <?php endforeach; ?>
```

```
    </div>
<?php else: ?>
    <p><?php echo t('There are no images!') ?></p>
<?php endif; ?>
```

Great. Now let's see what we did. At the very top of the file, of course, we included the `defined` or `die` statement that is required on all the PHP files. Following that, we load up the Image helper, which we will be using later to generate thumbnails.

Next, we output a title for the gallery, using the `t()` wrapper to remain translation friendly, of course.

Shortly after that, we begin looping through the array of images. These are `File` objects, so we have access to all of the related properties. Let's use the Image helper to generate a 100 x 100 pixel crop of the image (passing `true` as the second parameter tells the Image helper to crop the image, not just resize it). That will give our gallery a clean and consistent look.

Next, let's wrap the image in an `<a>` tag, so we can link to the full size image. Output the image tag, using the thumbnail's source.

Don't forget to wrap the whole thing in an `if` statement to handle file sets with no images.

Lastly, let's add some basic styles to `view.css` so our gallery looks pretty as follows:

```css
.gallery-wrapper {
  margin: 50px 0;
}

.gallery-image {
  opacity: .85;
}

.gallery-image:hover {
  opacity: 1;
}
```

Trying out the block

Alright, let's see how we did! Before we can use the block, let's add a file set to concrete5. Visit `/dashboard/files/sets/` in your browser and click on the big blue button to add a file set. We need to add at least one file set before we can use the gallery.

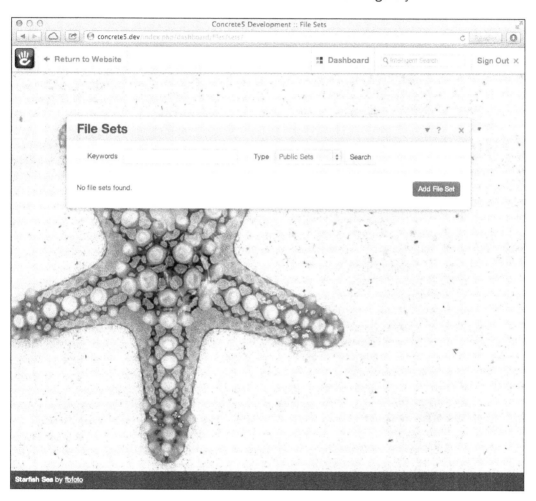

Create a new file set called `Gallery Images`.

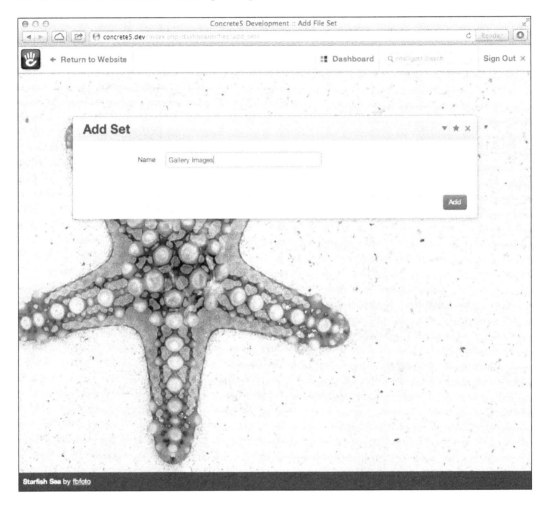

Now we have a file set, but still it is empty. Let's add some images to this file set by visiting the file manager at `/dashboard/files/search/`.

Select a few images to add to the set.

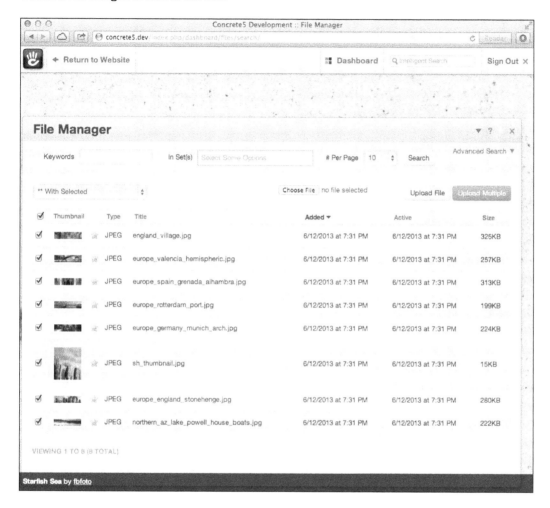

Click on the dropdown menu in the upper-left hand corner. Select **Sets**, as in the following screenshot:

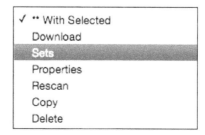

Select the file set that we just created to assign these images to that set.

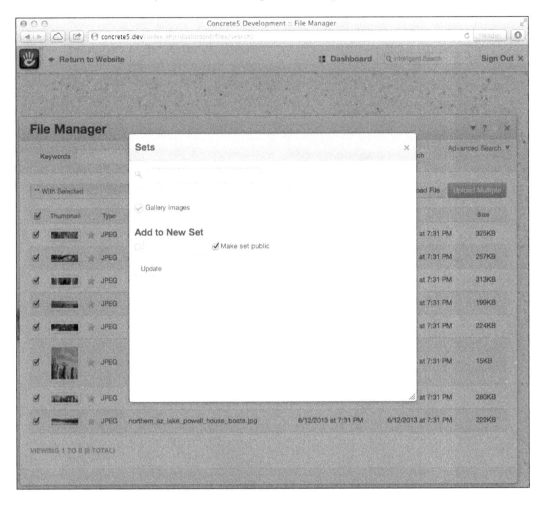

Fantastic! Now we are ready to try out our block. Visit the image gallery page that we created earlier and enter edit mode. Click on the main content area to add a new block.

Scroll to the bottom of the block list to find the photo gallery block that we created.

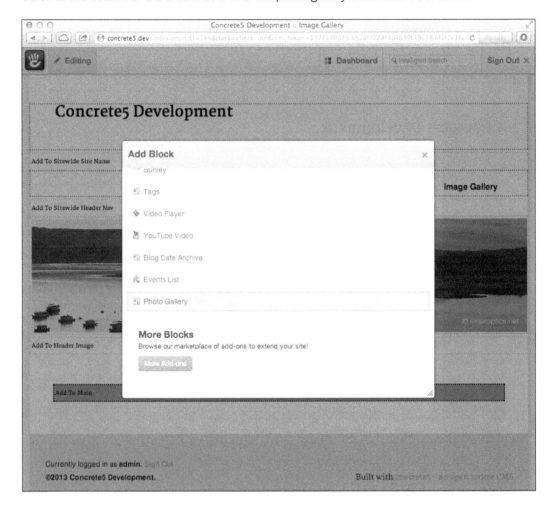

Now, fill out the form to add the block. Select the file set and set a limit to how many images can appear (or leave it blank to use the default of 20).

Add the block to the page and publish the changes. You will see a great-looking image gallery!

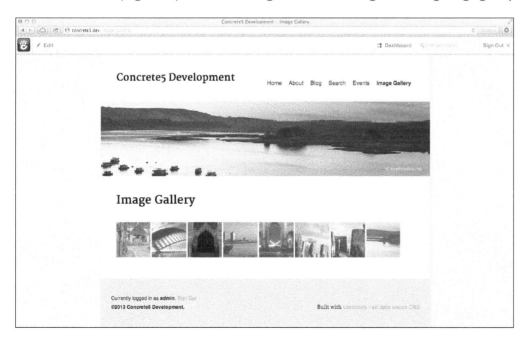

Click on one of the images to see it in its original size.

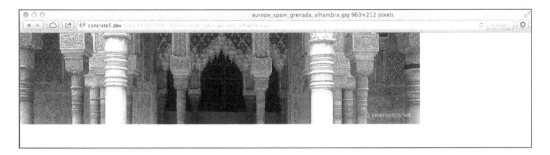

Well, that looks like our code worked! Congratulations, you have created an add-on that can be installed on any concrete5 website and work automatically.

Wrap-up

We accomplished a lot in this chapter. We started with nothing, and ended up with a fully functioning image gallery. There's still a lot of room for expansion and improvements, though. What if we would have added a jQuery lightbox plugin, such as fancyBox (available at `http://fancyapps.com/fancybox/`)? Or if the gallery had multiple pages? This block type is a great starting point for many different possibilities. These tasks are all possible with the concrete5 API, so have fun exploring and learning new things.

Blueprint – Creating an Events Calendar Add-on

Many add-ons that developers have to create end up combining dashboard interfaces and custom block types to not only provide great editing capabilities on the backend of the site, but also unique and powerful interfaces on the frontend of the website. A common request on websites is the ability to have an events calendar. This blueprint here is going to combine much of the knowledge that we gained in the prior chapters to create an events calendar add-on. The add-on will have a CRUD interface on the dashboard as well as a custom block type to display the events.

Before we begin...

Before we begin, we should note that the blueprint in this chapter is based on a fresh installation of concrete5, with all of the sample content loaded. This will give us some nice pages and a clean design to work with.

The complete working code for this add-on is available for free from the book's website. Feel free to download that as a starting point or to solve any problems you may run into.

Creating the package

Let's get moving. First, we will create the package's directory. Add a new directory in `/packages` called `cookbook_events`. Inside this directory, create the package's controller file.

The package controller

You may be familiar with package controllers already; they tell concrete5 about the package, as well as provide functionality for developers to perform advanced tasks.

Enter the following code in `controller.php`:

```php
<?php
defined('C5_EXECUTE') or die(_("Access Denied."));
class CookbookEventsPackage extends Package {
    protected $pkgHandle = 'cookbook_events';
    protected $appVersionRequired = '5.6.0.0';
    protected $pkgVersion = '0.9.0';
    public function getPackageName() {
        return t('Cookbook Events');
    }
    public function getPackageDescription() {
        return t('A calendar of events for our website.');
    }
}
```

Notice the use of the `defined or die` statement at the top of the file. This is required at the top of every PHP file in the package, otherwise concrete5 will reject your add-on if you submit it to the marketplace.

Also, note the use of the `t()` function around the package name and description strings. This will allow translators to offer translations of these strings in an easy and consistent way.

We are setting the minimum concrete5 Version to 5.6.0. as we are using some CSS styles that don't fully work on older versions of concrete5. With a little extra work, however, we could support older versions.

The package database XML file

Our package will need to create a database table to store the event data. Rather than executing raw SQL, the preferred methodology is to create a `db.xml` file that contains all of the tables and fields to be created. concrete5 will read this file when the package is installed and will perform the necessary database operations.

Create the `db.xml` file at `/packages/cookbook_events/db.xml`.

Enter the following XML code in the file:

```xml
<?xml version="1.0"?>
<schema version="0.3">
    <table name="CookbookEvents">
```

```xml
        <field name="id" type="I">
           <key />
           <unsigned />
           <autoincrement />
        </field>
        <field name="title" type="C" size="255"></field>
        <field name="event_date" type="T"></field>
        <field name="location" type="C" size="255"></field>
        <field name="description" type="X2"></field>
        <field name="created_by" type="I"></field>
        <field name="created_at" type="T"></field>
     </table>
  </schema>
```

Save this file. This tells concrete5 to create a table named `CookbookEvents`, with fields for a title, date, location, description, and some meta data. The use of `db.xml` also makes future database upgrades easier when your add-on is updated.

You may recall that this XML file makes use of the ADOdb XML schema format, or **AXMLS**. You can learn more about AXMLS and the different field types at `http://phplens.com/lens/adodb/docs-datadict.htm#xmlschema`.

The model

Now that we know what our database table looks like, let's create the model that we will use to interact with the table.

Create a new file at `/packages/cookbook_events/models/cookbook_event.php`.

Create the `model` class and specify the name of the database table:

```php
<?php
defined('C5_EXECUTE') or die(_("Access Denied."));
class CookbookEvent extends Model {
   var $_table = 'CookbookEvents';
    public function getDate() {
        return date(DATE_APP_GENERIC_MDY_FULL, strtotime($this->event_
date));
      }
}
```

Notice how we named the class `CookbookEvent` rather than just `Event`. This is to prevent collisions with other classes. Since `Event` is a fairly common name for a class, it is possible that there could be a conflict. It's always a good idea to make your class names as unique as possible, while still following convention and being easy to understand.

We also added a function to return a formatted version of the event's date. This will come in handy later.

Single page controllers

In order for our add-on to have interfaces on the dashboard, we will need to create a few single pages with controllers.

Create a file in `/packages/cookbook_events/controllers/dashboard/cookbook_events.php`. This is the root controller file for the add-on. Give it a basic class file:

```php
<?php
defined('C5_EXECUTE') or die(_("Access Denied."));
class DashboardCookbookEventsController extends Controller {
    public function on_start() {
        $this->redirect('/dashboard/cookbook_events/list');
    }
}
```

The `on_start` function will make sure that if anyone visits this page, they will be redirected to the default view showing the events listing. Let's create the controller for that view now.

Now create a new directory at `/packages/cookbook_events/controllers/dashboard/cookbook_events/`. Add two files to this directory: `add.php` and `list.php`.

In `list.php`, add the following class:

```php
<?php
defined('C5_EXECUTE') or die(_("Access Denied."));
class DashboardCookbookEventsListController extends Controller {
}
```

Great! Now in `add.php`, add another class:

```php
<?php
defined('C5_EXECUTE') or die(_("Access Denied."));
class DashboardCookbookEventsAddController extends Controller {
}
```

Looking good! Our single pages have basic controllers now, but they still need view files.

Single page views

Create the root view file for our interface at `/packages/cookbook_events/single_pages/cookbook_events.php`. Leave this file empty. Create a directory at `/packages/cookbook_events/single_pages/cookbook_events`. Add the two files, `add.php` and `list.php`, to this directory. We can leave these blank for now.

The event list block type

Before we can install our package, we need to make sure that the block type exists as well. This will allow us to automatically install the block type during the package's installation.

This block type that we are creating will show a list of the events that have been entered into the database. It will act as a basic agenda view for the site's events.

Create a new directory at `/packages/cookbook_events/blocks`. Now, create another directory in there called `cookbook_events`.

The first file that we will want to add to our block is the controller. Create `controller.php` in the block's directory.

Enter the following code in `controller.php`:

```php
<?php defined('C5_EXECUTE') or die(_("Access Denied."));
class CookbookEventsBlockController extends BlockController {
    protected $btTable = "btCookbookEvents";
    protected $btInterfaceWidth = "350";
    protected $btInterfaceHeight = "300";
    public function getBlockTypeName() {
        return t('Events List');
    }
    public function getBlockTypeDescription() {
        return t('A list of events!');
    }
}
```

Notice that we remembered to include the required `defined or die` statement at the top of the file. We'll continue prefixing our class names with `Cookbook` to allow our classes to avoid conflicting with existing classes.

We also defined the name of the database table that this block type will use. Let's create that table now using the database XML format.

The block's database XML file

Create a new file in the block directory named `db.xml`. Enter the following code in the XML file:

```xml
<?xml version="1.0"?>
<schema version="0.3">
    <table name="btCookbookEvents">
        <field name="bID" type="I">
            <key />
```

```
            <unsigned />
        </field>
        <field name="item_limit" type="I"></field>
    </table>
</schema>
```

This XML code will tell concrete5 to create a new table with two fields: a unique ID to identify the block, and a field to store how many events we want to display.

The block view files

If you recall from earlier chapters, blocks have three views that can be activated: add, edit, and view. Create `add.php`, `edit.php`, and `view.php` to represent each of these views. In our block, `add.php` and `edit.php` will show the same HTML, so we will create a fourth file for these views to share named `form.php`. Also, add a `view.css` file that will be used to apply styles to the frontend of the block.

Leave these files empty for now, as we are ready to install our block!

Installing the package

Open the package controller (located at `/packages/cookbook_events/controller.php`) in your code editor. Add a new method to the controller class named `install`. It should look like the following code snippet:

```php
public function install() {
    $pkg = parent::install();
    // Add the dashboard pages
    $mainPage = SinglePage::add('/dashboard/cookbook_events', $pkg);
    $listPage = SinglePage::add('/dashboard/cookbook_events/list',
$pkg);
    $addPage = SinglePage::add('/dashboard/cookbook_events/add',
$pkg);
    // install the block type
    BlockType::installBlockTypeFromPackage('cookbook_events', $pkg);
}
```

What's going on here? Well, if you recall, we created three single pages with controllers to be used for the dashboard interface. These pages will need to be added to the site map, so we hook into the package's installation routine to make sure that they get installed when the package is installed.

Next, we also install the block type. This will ensure that our block is available to use on the frontend of the website.

When concrete5 installs the package, it will run our package's `db.xml` file, creating the database tables defined in there. This will allow our package to remain completely portable, and it can be installed in any concrete5 website.

Let's install the package now.

Installing the package to the dashboard

Visit the package installation page on your concrete5 site, located at `/dashboard/extend/install/`. You should see the events package awaiting installation, as shown in the following screenshot:

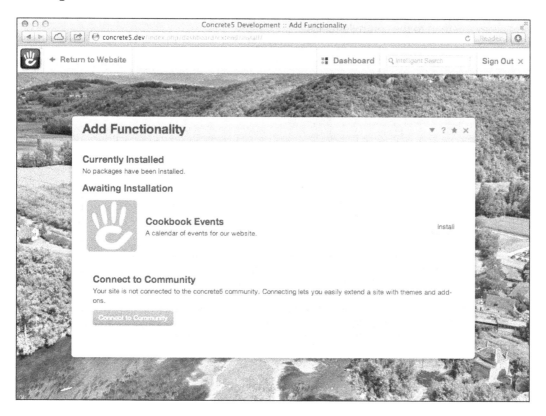

Click on the **Install** button on the package. If all goes well, the package will be installed! We should have some new pages on the dashboard, so visit `/dashboard/cookbook_events`.

Did you notice what happened? When we visit the `/dashboard/cookbook_events` page, it redirects us to `/dashboard/cookbook_events/list/`. This is intentional. The way that the dashboard is organized requires add-ons to have a parent page. That will allow our **Event List** and **Add Event** single pages to appear in the dashboard menu correctly.

This list page is still completely empty. Let's add some HTML to it and fill it out.

Creating the list single page

First, we will add some logic to the list page's controller file. Open `/packages/cookbook_events/controllers/dashboard/cookbook_events/list.php` in your code editor.

Add a view method to the controller class:

```php
public function view() {
    Loader::model('cookbook_event', 'cookbook_events');
    $event = new CookbookEvent();
    $events = $event->find('1=1 ORDER BY event_date');
    $this->set('events', $events);
}
public function delete($id = null) {
    if ($id) {
        Loader::model('cookbook_event', 'cookbook_events');
        $event = new CookbookEvent();
        $event->load('id = ?', $id);
        $event->delete();
        $this->redirect('/dashboard/cookbook_events/list?deleted');
    }
}
```

Remember that `view()` is one of the automatic callback functions that gets executed when the single page is viewed. Here, we are loading the `model` class that we created and are using it to find all instances of the events in the database. We then send the array of event objects to the view, using `$this->set()`.

We also added a function to delete events from the system, using the `model` class and active record.

Creating the list view

Let's open up the view and add some HTML to it. Open `/packages/cookbook_events/ single_pages/dashboard/cookbook_events/list.php` in your editor.

Add the following HTML code to the view file:

```php
<?php defined('C5_EXECUTE') or die(_("Access Denied.")); ?>
<div class="ccm-ui">

    <?php if (isset($_GET['success'])): ?>
        <div class="alert-message">
            <?php echo t('The event was saved successfully!') ?>
        </div>
    <?php endif; ?>
    <?php if (isset($_GET['deleted'])): ?>
        <div class="alert-message">
            <?php echo t('The event was deleted successfully!') ?>
        </div>
    <?php endif; ?>
    <div class="ccm-pane">
        <?php
            $dashboard = Loader::helper('concrete/dashboard');
            echo $dashboard->getDashboardPaneHeader(t('Events'));
        ?>
        <div class="ccm-pane-body">
            <?php if (!empty($events)): ?>
                <table class="table table-striped table-bordered">
                    <tr>
                        <th><?php echo t('Event ID') ?></th>
                        <th><?php echo t('Date') ?></th>
                        <th><?php echo t('Title') ?></th>
                        <th><?php echo t('Location') ?></th>
                        <th><?php echo t('Actions') ?></th>
                    </tr>
                    <?php foreach ($events as $event): ?>
                        <tr class="event-row">
                            <td><?php echo $event->id ?></td>
                            <td><?php echo $event->getDate() ?></td>
                            <td><?php echo $event->title ?></td>
                            <td><?php echo $event->location ?></td>
                            <td>
```

```
                              <a href="<?php echo $this->url('/dashboard/
cookbook_events/add/edit/', $event->id) ?>" class="btn"><?php echo
t('Edit') ?></a>
                                <a href="<?php echo $this->action('delete',
$event->id) ?>" class="btn danger delete"><?php echo t('Delete') ?></
a>
                        </td>
                    </tr>
                <?php endforeach; ?>
                </table>
            <?php else: ?>
                <p>
                    <?php echo t('There are no events! Add one now.'); ?>
                </p>
            <?php endif; ?>
        </div>
        <div class="ccm-pane-footer"></div>
    </div>
</div>
```

There's a lot here, but it's actually not too complex. First, we make sure to include the `defined or die` statement at the top of the file. Next, we output the header of the dashboard pane. This includes the controls to navigate around our add-on, as well as add the page to the main dashboard menu.

A little further down, we check to see if there's anything in the `$events` array. If there are, we can show the list of events in an HTML table. If there aren't, we will show a message to the user that there are no events in the system.

Next, we create an HTML table to hold the events. The table has five columns: the event ID, the event date, the title, location, and a column for some actions to be performed on the event.

Once we begin looping through the events array, we will output one table row for each event in the system. Each column in the event row will output the corresponding field on the event. Notice the use of the date getter function to output a nicely formatted date.

The last column contains the buttons to edit and delete an event. We added an additional CSS class of `.delete` to the **Delete** button that will allow us to use JavaScript to display a confirmation message. Let's save this file and refresh the page:

Looking good, except we don't have any events in our system yet. Let's create the form to add events.

Creating the add form single page

Open `/packages/cookbook_events/controllers/dashboard/cookbook_events/add.php` in your code editor. Let's add a few functions to this class:

```php
public function edit($id = null) {
    if ($id) {
        // in edit mode, load the event to be edited
        Loader::model('cookbook_event', 'cookbook_events');
        $event = new CookbookEvent();
        $event->load('id = ?', $id);
        // pass the event object to the view as an array
        $this->set('data', (array) $event);
    }
```

```
    }

    public function save() {
        $data = $_POST;
        // verify that all required fields have been filled out
        $val = Loader::helper('validation/form');
        $val->setData($data);
        $val->addRequired('title', t('Please enter a title.'));
        $passed = $val->test();
        if (!$passed) {
            $this->set('errors', $val->getError()->getList());
        }
        else {
            $dth = Loader::helper('form/date_time');
            Loader::model('cookbook_event', 'cookbook_events');
            $event = new CookbookEvent();
            if ($data['id']) {
                $event->load('id = ?', $data['id']);
            }
            $event->title = $data['title'];
            $event->event_date = $dth->translate('event_date');
            if ($data['location']) {
                $event->location = $data['location'];
            }
            if ($data['description']) {
                $event->description = $data['description'];
            }
            if (!$data['id']) {
                $user = new User();
                $event->created_by = $user->getUserID();
                $event->created_at = date('Y-m-d H:i:s');
            }
            $event->save();

            $this->redirect('/dashboard/cookbook_events/list?success');
        }
    }
```

First, we added a function to provide editing capabilities to this form. Essentially, if an ID is provided in the URL, we will use the event model to load the corresponding event and send it to the view as an array. We use an array because if the array is empty, the view will not produce errors as it would with an object.

Next, we define the function to actually save the new event. We use the Validation helper to verify that the required fields have been filled out. After that, we begin populating the event object to be saved to the database. One important thing to notice here is that we check for the presence of an event ID in the POST data. This is to allow us to edit an existing event, rather than create a duplicate one. We also use this area to set the metadata for the event, such as the ID of the user that added it, and the timestamp of when it was created.

Finally, we save the event object to the database and redirect the user back to the event list, displaying a success message.

The form view file

Of course, we still need to write the other half of this single page, the view. Let's open /packages/cookbook_events/single_pages/dashboard/cookbook_events/add.php and add the following HTML and PHP code to it:

```php
<?php
    defined('C5_EXECUTE') or die(_("Access Denied."));
    $form = Loader::helper('form');
    $dth = Loader::helper('form/date_time');

    Loader::element('editor_init');
    Loader::element('editor_config');
?>
<div class="ccm-ui">
    <?php if (!empty($errors)): ?>
        <div class="alert-message block-message error">
            <strong><?php echo t('There were some problems saving the event.') ?></strong>
            <ul style="margin-top: 5px;">
                <?php foreach ($errors as $e): ?>
                    <li><?php echo $e ?></li>
                <?php endforeach ?>
            </ul>
        </div>
    <?php endif; ?>
```

```php
<div class="ccm-pane">
    <?php
        $dashboard = Loader::helper('concrete/dashboard');
        echo $dashboard->getDashboardPaneHeader(t('Add Event'));
    ?>
    <form action=<?php echo $this->action('save') ?> method="POST">
        <div class="ccm-pane-body">
            <table class="table table-striped table-bordered">
                <tr>
                    <td class="form-label">
                        <?php echo t('Event Title') ?>
                        <span class="req">*</span>
                    </td>
                    <td>
                        <?php echo $form->text('title', $data['title'])
?>
                    </td>
                </tr>
                <tr>
                    <td class="form-label">
                        <?php echo t('Event Date') ?>
                        <span class="req">*</span>
                    </td>
                    <td>
                        <?php echo $dth->datetime('event_date',
$data['event_date']) ?>
                    </td>
                </tr>
                <tr>
                    <td class="form-label">
                        <?php echo t('Location') ?>
                    </td>
                    <td>
                        <?php echo $form->text('location',
$data['location']) ?>
                    </td>
                </tr>
                <tr>
```

```
                    <td class="form-label">
                        <?php echo t('Description') ?>
                    </td>
                    <td>
                        <?php
                            Loader::element('editor_controls');
                            echo $form->textarea('description',
$data['description'], array('style' => 'width:100%;', 'class' => 'ccm-
advanced-editor'));
                        ?>
                    </td>
                </tr>
            </table>
        </div>
        <div class="ccm-pane-footer">
            <div class="pull-right">
                <input type="submit" class="btn primary" value="<?php
echo t('Save Event') ?>">
                <a href="<?php echo $this->url('/dashboard/cookbook_
events/list') ?>" class="btn"><?php echo t('Cancel') ?></a>
            </div>
        </div>
        <?php if (!empty($data)): ?>
            <input type="hidden" name="id" value="<?php echo
$data['id'] ?>">
        <?php endif; ?>
    </form>
    </div>
</div>
```

Whoa, that's a lot of code! Don't worry, it's not as complex as it looks. At the top of the file, we of course add our `defined or die` statement, and then load two helpers, the Form helper and the Date field helper.

As our event's description field can contain HTML formatting, we will need to use a WYSIWYG editor. That editor needs some special JavaScript on the page before it can load, so we output that right away using the `editor_init` and `editor_config` elements.

Next, we begin our output by displaying any errors that occurred in the save procedure (for example, if the title field was left empty). After that, we use concrete5's Dashboard helper to output the header of the page, including the native page controls.

After that, we will define the form, setting the action of the form to use the `save` function in this page's controller and setting the HTTP method to `POST`.

Inside the form, we use a table to give our form a simple layout. We output fields for title, location, date, and description. At the bottom of the page, we display some buttons to save the data or to cancel and return to the events listing. Let's take a look at this form in our browser now!

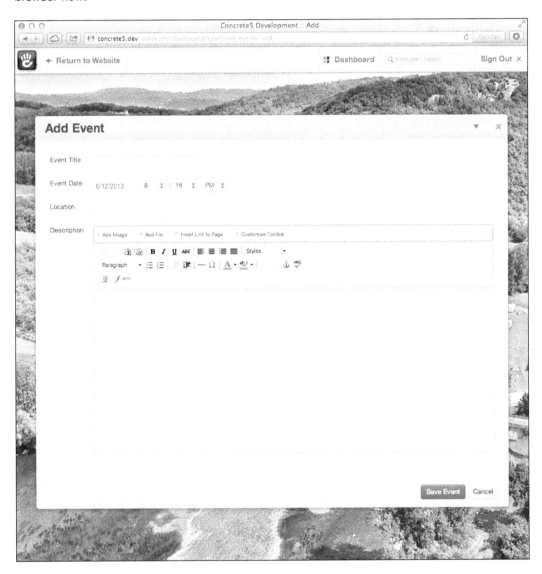

That looks great! Let's add a bunch of events to the site now, using this form.

Adding events to the database

Fill out the **Add Event** form that comes up with a couple of events to add to the database:

Once you have a few events entered, your list view should look something like the following:

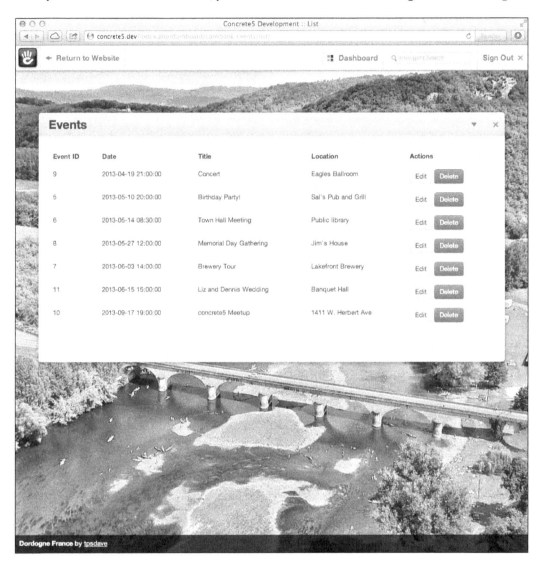

Looking great! Let's click on the **Delete** button on one of these events. It works, but users don't have any chance to cancel that action if they change their mind. We should use JavaScript to ask users if they are sure they want to delete the event.

Adding a delete confirmation

Let's add a new JavaScript file to /packages/cookbook_events/js/list.js. Add some JavaScript (using the jQuery library) to listen to the clicks on the **Delete** button:

```
$(document).ready(function() {
    $('.delete').on('click', function(e) {
        return confirm('Are you sure you want to delete this item?');
    });
});
```

Next, we need to make sure this script is included on our list page. Open up the controller for the list page located at /packages/cookbook_events/controllers/dashboard/cookbook_events/list.php.

Add a new function to include the JavaScript file on the page:

```
public function on_before_render() {
    $html = Loader::helper('html');
    $this->addHeaderItem($html->javascript('list.js', 'cookbook_
events'));
}
```

This function will use the HTML helper to automatically add the <script> tag to the page's <head> area.

Now, if you try to delete an event, you should see a confirmation dialog, as shown in the following screenshot:

Perfect! We can consider the backend of the add-on to be complete! All that is left to do is displaying events on the frontend.

Creating the custom block type

If you recall, we created some boilerplate files for our block type, but it doesn't actually do anything. We will want to create a block that shows a list of the events entered into the database.

First, let's add the HTML form to `form.php` that will be displayed whenever site editors add or edit the block on the site:

```php
<?php
defined('C5_EXECUTE') or die(_ ("Access Denied."));
$form = Loader::helper('form');
?>
<div class="ccm-ui">
    <table class="table table-striped table-bordered">
        <tr>
            <td>
                <?php echo t('Maximum events to show') ?>
            </td>
            <td>
                <?php echo $form->text('item_limit', $item_limit) ?>
            </td>
        </tr>
    </table>
</div>
```

Great! Let's include this file in both `add.php` and `edit.php`. Add the following to each of those files:

```php
<?php
defined('C5_EXECUTE') or die(_ ("Access Denied."));
include('form.php');
```

Alright! All we have to do now is create the frontend view of the block. Open `view.php` in your code editor and enter the following HTML and PHP code:

```php
<?php defined('C5_EXECUTE') or die(_ ("Access Denied.")); ?>
<h1 class="events-title"><?php echo t('Events Calendar') ?></h1>
<div class="events-list">
    <?php if (!empty($events)): ?>
        <?php foreach ($events as $event): ?>
            <div class="event-item">
                <h2><?php echo $event->title ?></h2>
                <div class="event-date">
                    <?php echo $event->getDate() ?>
                    <?php if ($event->location): ?>
```

```
                    @ <?php echo $event->location ?>
                <?php endif; ?>
            </div>
            <?php if ($event->description): ?>
                <div class="event-description">
                    <?php echo $event->description ?>
                </div>
            <?php endif; ?>
        </div>
    <?php endforeach; ?>
<?php else: ?>
    <p><?php echo t('There are no events!') ?></p>
<?php endif; ?>
</div>
```

That looks great! Here we are essentially looping through the $events array and displaying a row for each event. We again make use of the getDate() function on the event model to output a clean and friendly date.

Finally, let's add some simple CSS styles to view.css:

```
h1.events-title {
    margin-bottom: 30px !important;
}
.event-item {
    padding: 20px 0;
    border-bottom: 1px solid #ddd;
}
.event-item:last-child {
    border-bottom: 0;
}
.event-item p {
    margin: 0 !important;
}
.event-date {
    font-size: 12px;
    color: #888;
}
```

Nice! Now we are ready to see it in action!

Adding the block to a page

Create a new page on the site to hold the events:

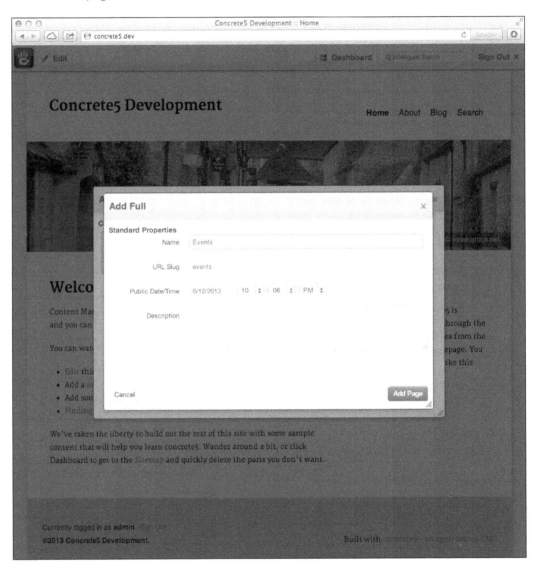

Add a new block to this page. Scroll down to the bottom of the blocks list to see the block that we have created:

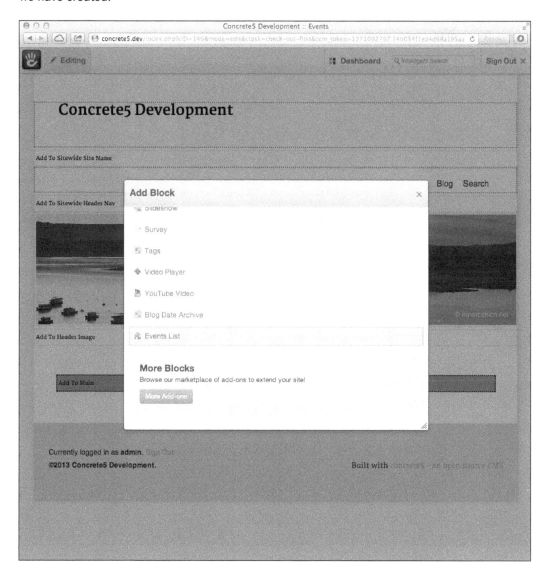

Fill out the form to add the block to the page. Set a limit for the amount of events to be displayed.

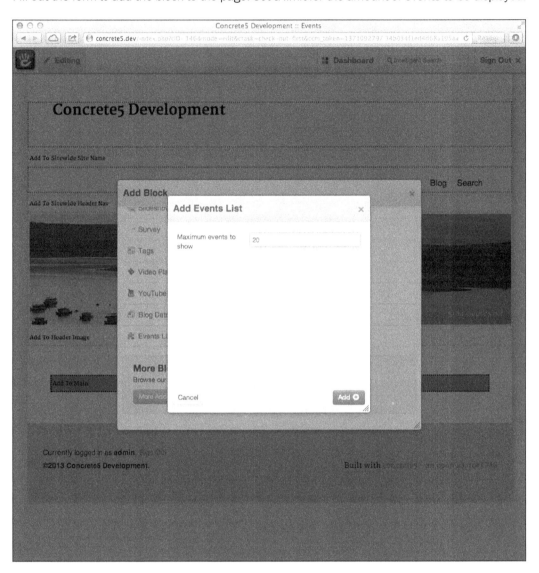

Now publish the changes on the page. You should see a handsome list of events!

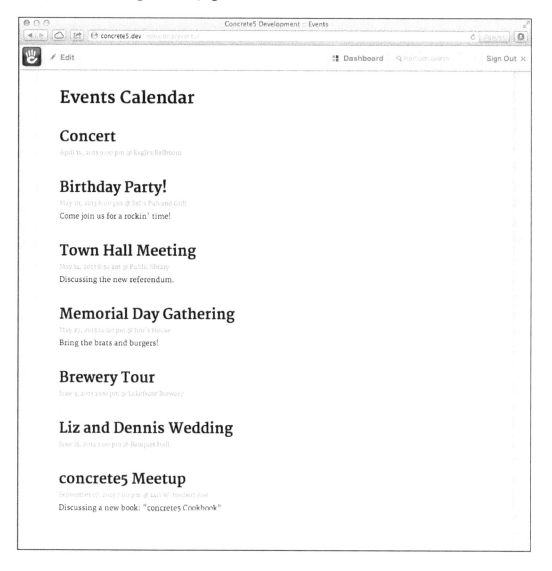

Wrapping up

Wow, we accomplished a lot! We started with absolutely nothing and built a fully functioning events calendar add-on. This add-on could be expanded to show alternate templates for the events, or to include advanced functionality such as hiding events that have already occurred, or giving each event its own page in the site map.

Hopefully this exercise has helped you get ideas on how to create packages for any need or situation.

Submitting an Add-on Package to the concrete5 Marketplace

Most content management systems have plugins or modules of some sort. concrete5 is fairly unique in that it comes with an entire ecosystem of add-ons and themes. This allows add-on developers to earn some money with the packages that they create for concrete5, and it also supports the concrete5 team, as concrete5 gets a percentage of each add-on that is sold.

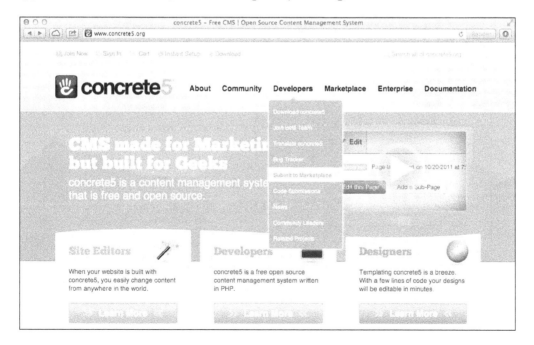

The rules

There are several rules that your add-on must adhere to. First and foremost, your add-on must work. There shouldn't be any errors while installing the add-on or while using it. Also, make sure that you own the rights to all of the code and assets contained within the add-on, or you have received proper permission from the code authors to include their code in your add-on.

Some other rules include using `defined or die` statements at the top of every PHP file, including an icon, and making sure to wrap all strings in the global `t()` function. Add-on developers are also expected to support their add-on and release updates to fix bugs and address customer complaints.

There are many more tips and rules posted on the concrete5 website at `http://www.concrete5.org/developers/marketplace-submission-rules/`.

The process

When submitting a package to the concrete5 marketplace, first you will need an account on `www.concrete5.org`. Once you have created an account, you will have to fill out a form (located at `http://www.concrete5.org/marketplace/manage_item/`) containing information about your package:

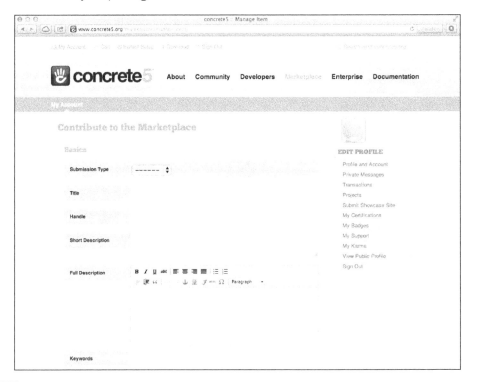

You will fill out all of the marketing copies that will appear in the marketplace listing, as well as some internal meta data about your add-on.

Once you have submitted the add-on, some automated tests will be performed on it to see if it meets the eligibility requirements. Once the add-on passes these tests, members of the **Peer Review Board** (**PRB**) will take a look at your add-on.

The Peer Review Board

The PRB is a group of volunteers from the concrete5 community. These volunteers are responsible for testing every add-on and theme that is submitted to the marketplace. They will install your package on their own version of concrete5 and test it fully to make sure it will work without difficulties, and to ensure that your add-on adheres to the rules.

Selling your add-on

concrete5 allows developers to sell their add-on. The lowest price you can set for an add-on (other than free) is $15 USD. concrete5 will keep 25 percent of your add-on's revenue, but the exposure they provide to your add-on by featuring it in the marketplace is usually worth a small commission.

If you sell an add-on in the concrete5 marketplace, you will be expected to support it. If your add-on doesn't work and you do not provide support for it, concrete5 will refund the customer and also charge you a 15 percent penalty. Make sure you are prepared to invest the time in supporting your add-ons.

Once the add-on is approved...

If your add-on passes the review board and is approved, it will be listed as available in the concrete5 marketplace. Be sure to pay attention to customer inquiries or support requests. Also, if you are selling your add-on, remember to request payments for downloads on a regular basis.

Official resources

The following links are recommended for developers interested in selling their themes and add-ons:

- ▸ The marketplace rules can be found at `http://www.concrete5.org/developers/marketplace-submission-rules/`.

- ▸ Tips for getting your add-on approved by the PRB can be found at `http://www.concrete5.org/documentation/how-tos/developers/why-do-marketplace-submissions-take-time-to-get-through-the-prb/`.

- ▸ concrete5 coding style guidelines can be found at `http://www.concrete5.org/documentation/developers/system/coding-style-guidelines`.

Index

TinyMCE 99

U

uID attribute 28
update function 29
URL Helper
  used, for generating URLs 108, 109
URLs
  generating, with URL Helper 108, 109
user
  adding, to group 167
  attributes, retrieving 164, 165
  attributes, setting 162-164
  currently logged-in user, getting 159
  deleting 171
  file permissions, checking 175
  getting, from group 168
  group member status, checking 168, 169
  info, getting 161, 162
  loading, by ID 159, 160
  loading, by user name 160, 161
  logging out 170, 171
  log in status, checking 158
  page editing capability, checking 174
  page reading capability, checking 173
  removing, from group 169, 170

UserInfo class 161
UserInfo object 164
username
  user, loading by 160, 161

V

Validation helpers
  used, for validating input data 109, 110
var_dump function 7
variables
  sending, from controller to view 54, 55
view
  creating, to display database items
    list 151, 152
  files, creating for single pages on
    dashboard 144, 145
view function 230
view() function 53

W

white label CMS
  concrete5, rebranding as 213, 214
WYSIWYG editor
  including, in form 99, 100

Thank you for buying
concrete5 Cookbook

About Packt Publishing

Packt, pronounced 'packed', published its first book "*Mastering phpMyAdmin for Effective MySQL Management*" in April 2004 and subsequently continued to specialize in publishing highly focused books on specific technologies and solutions.

Our books and publications share the experiences of your fellow IT professionals in adapting and customizing today's systems, applications, and frameworks. Our solution based books give you the knowledge and power to customize the software and technologies you're using to get the job done. Packt books are more specific and less general than the IT books you have seen in the past. Our unique business model allows us to bring you more focused information, giving you more of what you need to know, and less of what you don't.

Packt is a modern, yet unique publishing company, which focuses on producing quality, cutting-edge books for communities of developers, administrators, and newbies alike. For more information, please visit our website: www.packtpub.com.

About Packt Open Source

In 2010, Packt launched two new brands, Packt Open Source and Packt Enterprise, in order to continue its focus on specialization. This book is part of the Packt Open Source brand, home to books published on software built around Open Source licences, and offering information to anybody from advanced developers to budding web designers. The Open Source brand also runs Packt's Open Source Royalty Scheme, by which Packt gives a royalty to each Open Source project about whose software a book is sold.

Writing for Packt

We welcome all inquiries from people who are interested in authoring. Book proposals should be sent to author@packtpub.com. If your book idea is still at an early stage and you would like to discuss it first before writing a formal book proposal, contact us; one of our commissioning editors will get in touch with you.

We're not just looking for published authors; if you have strong technical skills but no writing experience, our experienced editors can help you develop a writing career, or simply get some additional reward for your expertise.

Joomla! 2.5 Beginner's Guide

ISBN: 978-1-84951-790-4   Paperback: 426 pages

An easy to use step-by-step guide to creating perfect websites with the free Joomla! CMS

1. Create a Joomla! website in an hour with the help of easy-to-follow steps and screenshots

2. Go beyond a typical Joomla! site to make a website that meets your specific needs

3. Learn how to secure, administrate, and fill your site with content

4. Update to the popular Joomla! 1.5 Beginner's Guide by Eric Tiggeler

Creating Concrete5 Themes

ISBN: 978-1-78216-164-6   Paperback: 160 pages

Create high quality concrete5 themes using practical recipes and responsive to make it mobile-ready

1. Get to grips with the concrete5 architecture

2. Learn how to create a concrete5 theme

3. Discover how to make a theme responsive to improve it for small devices

Please check **www.PacktPub.com** for information on our titles

concrete5 Beginner's Guide

ISBN: 978-1-84951-428-6   Paperback: 320 pages

Create and customize your own website with the concrete5 Beginner's Guide

1. Follow the creation of a sample site, through the installation, configuration, and deployment of a Concrete5 site

2. Use themes and add-ons to create a personalized site

3. Ideal introduction to using the Concrete5 CMS

4. Part of Packt's Beginner's Guide series – lots of practical examples, screenshots, and less of the waffle

RapidWeaver 5 Beginner's Guide

ISBN: 978-1-84969-205-2   Paperback: 362 pages

Build beautiful and professional websites with ease using RapidWeaver

1. Jump into developing websites on your Mac with RapidWeaver

2. Step-by-step tutorials for novice users to get your websites built and published online

3. Advanced tips and exercises for existing RapidWeaver users

4. A great A-Z guide for building websites irrespective of your level of expertise

Please check **www.PacktPub.com** for information on our titles

www.ingramcontent.com/pod-product-compliance
Lightning Source LLC
Chambersburg PA
CBHW060519060326
40690CB00017B/3321